THE KOLAM TRIBALS

Castes and Tribes of India Series

1. The Korku Tribals/**S.G. Deogaonkar** and **Shailaja S. Deogaonkar.**
2. Socio-cultural Study of Scheduled Tribes: The Pardhans of Maharashtra/**S.R. Murkute.**
3. The Banjara/**S.G. Deogaonkar** and **Shailaja S. Deogaonkar**.
4. Mythos and Logos of the Warlis : A Tribal Worldview/Compiled by Avellino Remedies Edited by *Ajay Dandekar* Foreword by **Rudolf C. Heredia**.
5. Naga Cultural Attires and Musical Instruments/ **Kajen Mongra, A Lanu Ao** (Ed.)
6. Ethnography of a Nomadic Tribe : A Study of Yanadi/ **N. Sudhakar Rao**.
7. The Kolam Tribals/**S.G. Deogaonkar** and **Leena Deogaonkar-Baxi.**
8. The Tribal Dance and Songs/**S.G. Deogaonkar** and **Shailaja S. Deogaonkar**

About the Authors

S.G. Deogaonkar is a retired Reader in Political Science, holding Master Degrees in Political Science and Public Administration and a Ph.D. degree in Social Science. He also holds an LL.M. degree in Constitutional Law. A scholar of repute, he has completed about ten post-doctoral research projects and has about fifteen books to his credit based on his research, mostly based on field-work.

Dr. Deogaonkar specialises in Political Anthropology and Tribal Development and has been associated with various State level as well as National level bodies and committees of the concerned Governments on Tribal Development.

For the last fifteen years he was a Non-official Member in the Governing Council of the Tribal Research & Training Institute, Maharashtra State (Pune) and for ten years was Member of the Zonal Advisory Council for the Western Zone of the Life Insurance Corporation of India. Recently he was Member of the Expert Committee appointed by the Maharashtra State for re-verification of entries of Tribal communities in the State Governments Resolution of 1985.

He is also a social worker working amidst tribal populations since the last twenty-five years. He is associated with many Voluntary Organisations working in tribal areas. He has published research papers in Journals and has presented papers at University as well as National and International Conferences and Seminars.

Some of his reputed books include. The Madia of Bhamragad, the Korku Tribals, the Banjara, The Hill Korwa, Tribal Exploitation, Tribal Development Plans; etc.

Leena S. Deogaonkar (alias Mrs. Leena Anirudh Baxi) is an Advocate practising at Bombay High Court at Mumbai. She is an LL.M. in Constitutional Law and for some time was a lecturer in Law, at the Government Law College, Churchgate, Mumbai. She has studied the problems of Law and Justice in some tribal societies from Maharashtra State.

Castes and Tribals of India Series No. 7

THE KOLAM TRIBALS

S.G. DEOGAONKAR

LEENA DEOGAONKAR-BAXI

CONCEPT PUBLISHING COMPANY, NEW DELHI-110059

ISBN 81-8069-011-3

First Published 2003

Published and Printed by
Ashok Kumar Mittal
Concept Publishing Company
A/15-16, Commercial Block, Mohan Garden
New Delhi-110059 (INDIA)

Phones : 25351460, 25351794
Fax : 091-11-25357103
Email : publishing@conceptpub.com.

PREFACE

The Kolam is yet another tribe in Maharashtra which has been classified as a 'primitive' tribe. These tribals are concentrated in the Nanded, Kinwat and Yavatmal districts of the State and has its spill over in the Chandrapur district. Their presence is also traced in the adjacent parts of Andhra Pradesh with slightly different nomenclature. Due to our association with tribal research projects we came in contact with the Kolam and were impressed by their cultural similarities with the Gonds, as well as their identity as a separate tribe adopting many culture traditions from the surrounding non-tribal Hindu traditions.

Economic conditions of the Kolam are significantly very poor. Absence of political leadership was also another feature which contributed to their backwardness. They have still maintained their traditional Panchayat system and have been solving most of their disputes within their community though they are surrounded by urbanity which is a court-addict society. All these features attracted us to the study of the tribe. Their folk-literature was also found to be very rich in content. All these factors have been studied in the present study of this tribe.

Shri Shriram Zode from Kolam village Pijdura and his team of Kolam youths which prominently included Shri Masram, Shri Atram and others have done a good job in collecting information and in canvassing the returns. Shri Milind Khelkar, Shri C.R. Watkar, Prof. Patingrao, Shri Sandeep Thakur participated in the field investigation work in Rajura and Korapna tahsils. The Kolam elders form the Yavatmal and Chandrapur district have also been very helpful. We thank all of them.

Dr. Mrs. Shailaja Deogaonkar has made valuable contributions to this book; for which I express my gratitude to her.

S.G. Deogaonkar

Leena Deogaonkar-Baxi

CONTENTS

LIST OF PLATES

1

THE KOLAM AND THEIR HABITAT

The Kolam

The Kolam tribals mainly found in the Yavatmal, Chandrapur, Nanded and Kinwat districts of Maharashtra State and in adjacent parts of Andhra Pradesh and Madhya Pradesh are classified as a Scheduled Tribe and in Maharashtra recognised as a primitive tribe by the Government of India. In Maharashtra State there are in all three tribes recognised as primitive *viz*. the Madia-Gonds in the Chandrapur-Gadchiroli district, the Katkaris in Thane district and the third group is of the Kolam tribals. The Kolam are grouped in the Dravidian group of tribes and are ethnically and culturally akin to the Gonds. But they display some characteristics which are dis-similar to the Gonds and the Pardhans who are juxtaposed with the Kolam in Yavatmal district.

Habitat

The Kolam are treated as a scheduled tribe in the Vidarbha and Marathwada regions of Maharashtra State. It has also been declared as a primitive tribe in the State. Their main habitat in Vidarbha is found in the Chandrapur, Yavatmal districts while they are also found in the Kinwat, Nanded and Osmanabad districts of Marathwada. It is a scheduled tribe in Madhya Pradesh also but the population is not significant. In Yavatmal they are concentrated in the Kelapur, Wani and Maregaon tehsils and usually are found on the hill slopes and forests. The spill over of the tribe from Yavatmal district accounts for the Kolam villages in Warora tehsil and Rajura tahsil of the Chandrapur district. In Warora they are mainly found in Pijdura, Mangli and Dindoda and in about 31 villages from the Rajura and Korapna tehsils.

Traditionally they prefer to stay away from the non-tribal population of the area. As such the Kolam *Pod* is either an independent unit or an annex to some non-tribal village. Hence, a Kolam village is identified as a *Pod.*

Population of the Kolam

The following figures from the 1981 census indicate a high concentration of the Kolam tribals in Maharashtra State.

Table 1.1: Kolam tribals: High Concentration

	Males	*Females*	*Total*
Maharashtra	59,301	58,772	1,18,073
Madhya Pradesh	160	139	299

The 1991 census figures indicate that their population has increased to 1,47,591. Table 1.2 gives a comparative picture of the populations of three primitive tribes in Maharashtra State.

Table 1.2: Primitive Tribe Population in Maharashtra State

Name of the Primitive Tribe	*Census Figures for*			
	1961	*1971*	*1981*	*1991*
Katkari	1,35,839	1,46,785	1,74,602	2,18,253
Kolam	43,555	56,061	1,18,073	1,47,591
Madia-Gond (Estimated)	2,22,114	2,56,246	3,59,425	4,49,281

Note: In 1991 Census, no separate Tribe-wise population figures were provided. Mentioned here are provisional 1991 census figures worked out on the basis of general growth rate of 2.5% per year.

Source: Tribal Research & Training Institute, Maharashtra State, Pune, *vide* their letter No. TRTI/1097/Pra.Kra./Ka-5/2618, dated 14/17-7-1998.

Identification of the Tribe

The Kolam are also identified as *Metlokur, Mannerwarlu* or *Mughlaikul.* They believe that their race has originated from the Pandavas of the Great Mahabharat and call themselves *Pandav-Vanshi.* They also consider their racial origin from the roots of Tamarind tree.

Identification of one's own tribe is always a sensitive issue. Ethnocentric considerations are often found which create hurdles in self-identification. Particularly in case of the Kolam, the tribe is scattered over a large geographical area spread in parts of Andhra Pradesh, Maharashtra and Madhya Pradesh and for geographical and other reasons, have lost contacts with each other. Even the groups found in Maharashtra State, *i.e.* in Yavatmal and Chandrapur have very few contacts over the last fifty years. They are so much engrossed in earning their bread that they have few occasions to meet. All this has resulted in the erosion of identity with their counterparts living in distant habitats in the same State.

For example the Yavatmal and Chandrapur Kolams have little contacts with those in Nanded and Kinwat and their cultural characteristics also diverge.

Their Conception about the Status of the Tribe

The Kolam consider themselves superior to the Gonds, Pardhan, Mang and Boudha, and inferior to Kunbis, Telis, etc. Even among themselves 4 and 7 God-groups are superior while others are inferior. Within these two, some consider 4 God-group superior and 7 God-group inferior, while some other Kolams consider 7 God-group superior and 4 God-group inferior.

Some Kolams stated that they are superior to the Gonds and Pardhans, while some other consider themselves as superior to the Pardhans while inferior to the Gonds. But all of them stated that they are superior to the Scheduled Caste like the Mahar, Mang etc. and inferior to the Brahmins, Telis, Kunbis etc.

The Kolam have a high sense of status and prestige as against other tribes and consider themselves ethnically related to the Pandvas (*Pandav–Vanshi*) of the *Mahabharat.*

Their love for their tribe and culture is also reflected in the fact that they are very conscious and proud of their socio-cultural traditions and follow all their rituals meticulously. Due to the work of Christian Missionaries, there has been some impact of Christianity on the population of the Yavatmal district but there are very few conversions among Kolams. Similarly in Yavatmal and Chandrapur districts many have accepted Buddhism but the percentage of Kolams turning to Buddhism is almost negligible. They are true to their Kolami religion.

Migration

In Maharashtra State they are mainly found in the Yavatmal and the Chandrapur districts. The Kolams in the Chandrapur district have migrated from the Yavatmal district some 50 to 60 years ago. In most of the returns from Mangli in the Chandrapur district, they mentioned that they came from the villages, namely:

> Paraskund, Sonurli, Botoni, Dahegaon, Kinhi, Buranda (Gond) Shivarni, Jathimathani, Kumbha, Jambhulni, Rampur, Karanji Baiba and Babhulgaon. (All from Yavatmal)

Various clan groups are found spread over the villages studied. In some villages they have emigrated 50 to 60 years back from other places. This applies particularly to the villages from Chandrapur district, namely- Mangli, Pijdura, Dindoda and a small establishment near Nandori. The Nandori Kolams have migrated from Salebhatti, Pijgaon, Babaipol, Jambe, Jalka (Bazar), Rale-gaon, Shivani, Sarathi, Raipur, Kinshi (Forest) etc. The Metlokur found in Nandori trace their origin to Pandavas and consider their clans origin from the roots of Tamarind tree. They are alternatively called as Mannerwarku, or Mannerlu, Mannerwarlu. (They do use all these three terms in the manner spelt above).

The Dindoda Kolams have migrated from Kinhi, Deodhari, Sakki, Wadhona, Pawra, Arvi, Rairi, etc.

The Pijdura Kolams have migrated from Botoni, Rampur, Pandharadevi, Jalka, Maregaon, Kumbha, Sonurli, Dahegaon, Ghantanj, Hivari, Babhulgaon, Nagara, Matharjun.

All these places are from Yavatmal district, and they stated that they came for labour work.

It seems that between 1910 to 1950, from Yavatmal district they migrated to these villages from Warora tehsil of the Chandrapur district as labourers doing the work of stone cutting and settled down near the work site. Some other Kolams migrated to the Manikgarh area of the Rajura tehsil and more so to the Korapna tehsil which was previously a part of Adilabad district before States Reorganisation. Even in Warora, Dindoda and Nandori Kolams have migrated much later as compared to the Pijdura and Mangli Kolams.

In the returns from Yavatmal district the following places were reported as their original habitats. Most of them migrated for getting labour work.

Gautala, Jambe, Matni, Sharari, Babai, Salebhatti, Kinhi, Sawarkheda, Ghubadyeti, Subhashyeti, Ghugaldara, Krishnapur, Goddhara, Shivni, Deodhari, Digdoh, Singaldeep, Vihirgaon, Dahegaon, Sonurli, Babhulgaon, Gargoti-pod, Bandar, Aawalgaon, Pandavpira,

Jalka, Mughuldhara, Mukutban, Kayar, Matharjun, Parsoda, Buranda, Munjala, Mahagaon, Jari-Jamni, Pandharadevi, Vihirgaon, Ambezari, Vegaon, Bhalewadi, Dongargaon, Rohpat, Khemkund, Nagara, Sawangi, Belori, Salaipol, Babay etc.

The Kolam from the Rajura and Korapna tehsils of Chandrapur district reported that they migrated from the adjoining areas from Andhra Pradesh, with which it has state border (List of Kolam villages from Rajura and Korapna tehsils is given below).

List of Villages Inhabited by Kolam Tribals, Distt. Chandrapur

Rajura and Korapna Tehsils	Warora Tehsil
1. Nagapur	29. Pijdura (Kolam *Pod*)
2. Sitaguda	30. Mangli
3. Bhoksapur	31. Dindoda
4. Yellapur	
5. Bhaipathar	
6. Hirapur	
7. Tatakohad	
8. Nokewada	
9. Bhuri Yesapur	
10. Chikhli Bujrug	
11. Shengaon	
12. Patan	
13. Matadi	
14. Lambori	
15. Nandpa	
16. Pittiguda	
17. Lasmaguda	
18. Maharajguda	
19. Ambezari	
20. Jivti	
21. Marai-Patan	
22. Pallezari	
23. Machchiguda	
24. Dharampur-Mohda	
25. Kawadgondi	
26. Marka Meta	
27. Sagnapur	
28. Ganeri	

Social Organisation

Ethnic Origin

R.V. Russell and Hiralal[1] have described the Kolam as a Dravidian tribe residing principally in the Wani taluka (now divided into Wani, Kelapur and Maregaon talukas) of Yavatmal district. Accepting Mr. Hislop's view they also opined that this tribe is akin to the Gonds. Mr. Hislop mentions that the Kolam extend all along the Kandi-Konda or Pindi hills on the South of the Wardha river. Their presence in the Wardha district was also mentioned by him.

The Chandrapur Gazetteer of 1909 does not report the presence of the Kolam tribe.[2] However, the second revised edition of the Gazetteer of 1973 reported presence of the Kolam tribe and quoted the figures of the 1961 census showing 778 males and 738 females in the district.[3] Thus the Kolam tribals have migrated to the district during the last sixty years.

It seems, between 1910 to 1950 they migrated to the adjoining Warora tehsil of the Chandrapur district as labourers doing the work of stone-cutting and formed their localities. Some of them also migrated to the Manikgarh area of the Rajura tehsil which was a part of the Adilabad district of Andhra Pradesh before States Reorganisation. According to 1961 census the only Kolam establishments shown in Warora tehsil were at Mangli and Pijdura.[4] And there is no mention of Dindoda which seems to be later development. Hence, living apart the Kolams in Rajura and Korapna which were included in Chandrapur district due to Reorganisation of States, the Kolam *Pods* (villages) at Mangli, Pijdura and Dindoda appear to be the only establishments due to the migration of Kolams from Yavatmal district.

Social Position and Organisation

As pointed out above, Mr. Hislop observes that the Kolams are akin to Gonds. They retain some very primitive customs. Colonel Mackenzie notes that they are held to be lower than the Gonds, because a Kolam will take food from a Gond, but the latter will not return the compliment.[5] They eat the flesh of rats, tigers, snakes, squirrels but they do not eat dogs, donkeys and jackals.

They are divided into four groups *Kula Gats*, (phratries) namely, *Char Deve* (worshippers of four Gods), *Pach Deve* (those who worship five Gods), *Saha Deve* (those who worship six Gods), and *Sat Deve* (those who worship seven Gods). A boy from one group cannot marry a girl from the same group and vice versa, *i.e.* for marriage purpose the group (*Kulgat*) of the bride and bridegroom must be different. Two and half God-group was also reported but was rare.

The Basis for Social Organisation

Consanguinity is the basis of their social organisation.

The important phratries among the Kolams are based on the number of Gods worshipped by the clans/septs included in the phratry. This is similar to the Gonds. The important Gond-groups and the major clans included in them are as follows:

God-group (Phratries)	*Clans/Septs: (Gotras)*
2½ Gods	Kove, Sekke, Veergama
4 Gods	* Tekam, Kumre, Bhurkhi
5 Gods	*Tekam, Yedse, Bhose, Rampur, Surpam, Kumraker, Jaruvare, Ramgade, Dawane
6 Gods	Atram, Sukli, Ravi, Siley, Kovakul, Zode, Wagdhare, Khadse, Borkar, Jambe, Maregama, Borgama, Khedki, Kovaker, Dhasalkar, Vadda, Zari, Deonare, Pidigama, Kodape, Gezrak, Dhoble Mundali, Jambhulkar, Baiba, Ghatanji, Anji, Vadhona
7 Gods	Meshram, Masram, Kergama, Vedsi, Madavi, Dhabadi, Savanji, Raddi, Kinare, Lonsavle, More, Junghare

* It is interesting to note that Tekam is common in the 4 and 5 God-groups. This is not similar to the Gonds.

Different Clan Names

Among the Kolams in the region the clan names are being used as surnames but there have been additions to these names. As a result many new surnames synonymous with or derived from clan names have been recorded.

Bhurkhi, Kelki, Lakhu, Vergama, Parandekul, Shiley Shilekar, Aanzi, Vadang, Bhurchi, Vedsi, Kanni, Velsokul, Zankul, Jaruvare, Reddi, Gereveddi, Khedki, Bondi, Ghatanji, Tikhandi, Konde, Moryak Merey, Shivni, Bhose, Maregama, Botoni, Bayaba, Zari, Bochche, Mangurle, Ravi, Rampure, Kergama, Kodape, Zode, Khadse, Bode,

Lumchyak, Deotare, Lonekar, Vadoda, Madavi, Sekke, Bhodekar, Aiengapure, Aanji, Yelki, Aaswale, Vala, Mundali, Vadda, Masgi, Surpam, Tikandi, Jambe, Vadekar, Kergama, Zambkol, Bhikund, Veergama, Nimma, Dhabadi, Kovekar, Kumraker, Villari, Gezrak, Pidigama, Doble, Kinnare, Shivnare, Tekam, Dawane, Janagi, Loni, Bhuvare, Korzare, Rampuryak, Waghadhara, Tumkod, Kodape, Borgama, Lonsawle, Raddi, Jambhulkar, Ghotekar, Metkar, Mangi, Gochchi, Kirkari, Mangurle, Nimmi, Kowa, Kikkadhari, Torambe, Kelgundi, Yelki, Verna, Ghate, Vadade, Waghade, Rengamuryak, Shelukar, Mundale, Atram, Zabkol, Tumchok, Parande, Dhobryak, Gobri, Khani, Sari, Geregaddi, Mohre, Shivnare, Ghate.

Russel and Hiralal had recorded 50 sept-names in Kolam and opined that only one *i.e.*, Tekam is found among the Gonds. However, in the present study many more (about 114) sept-names have been reported and the following are common even among the Gonds. These are : Tekam, Atram, Kowe, Kumre, Masram, Kodape.

Symbols of the Septs

The Kolams reported various symbols for different septs. These include animals, vegetables and other objects.

Animals : Tiger, Dog, Goat, Sheep, Buffalo, Cow, Pig

Vegetables : Paddy, Sugarcane, Carrot, Brinjal, Ambadi, Methi (leafy vegetables)

Before eating such vegetables, they are first worshipped (Puja), and then eaten.

REFERENCES

1. Russell and Hiralal, *Tribes and Castes of the Central Provinces of India,* Vol. III, Cosmo Publications, Delhi, 1973, p. 520.
2. Gazetteer of India, Chandrapur District Gazetteer, Maharashtra State, First Edition, 1909, p. 159.
3. *Ibid.* Second Revised Edition, 1973, p. 437.
4. Mandaokar, Bhau, *'Kolam'*, Seva Publications, Amravati, 1966, p. 30.
5. Russell and Hiralal, *'Tribes and Castes of the Central Provinces of India,'* Vol. III, Cosmo Publications, Delhi, 1979, p. 524.

2

CULTURE

Physical Culture

Physical Characteristics

They are usually dark in complexion and possess more or less the same characteristics as the Andhs and Kunbis who are their neighbours in cultivation.

The anthropometric indices for the Kolam are as given below[1].

		m.m.
1.	Head (circumference)	527.90
	Ratio/Cephalic index	76.13
2.	Nose height	108.57
	Ratio of length and width of nose	86.41
3.	Length of upper jaw	45.32
4.	Ratio of the width of face and head	95.85

In racial characteristics they come closer to the other tribes in the region which are of Dravidian origin. This fact is also corroborated by their Kolami dialect which Grierson found similar to that of the Naik Gonds of Chandrapur district. Hence, ethnically they are nearer to the other Dravidian tribe.

The Chandrapur Gazetteer of 1909 does not report the presence of the Kolam tribe, however the second review edition of 1973 reported presence of Kolam tribe and quoted the figures of the 1961 census showing 778 males and 738 females in the district. Thus the Kolam tribals have migrated to the district during the last sixty years. The returns from Kolam villages around Warora have also confirmed this fact.

Food Habits

They take vegetarian as well as non-vegetarian food. The staple food consists of juar and may be supplemented by wheat, rice etc. They eat meat of all animals including pigs and occasionally even beef is eaten. Many other birds and animals are also eaten. They eat all vegetables including Ambadi, Math (Toṭa kusse), Kumbha and other seasonal vegetables like cabbages, brinjals and roots like carrot, radish etc. They also eat fruits like banana, guava, oranges, mangoes, ziziphus, cucumber etc. They also consume milk, tea and occasionally coffee.

Liquor consumption is very common. Mostly country liquor is consumed. After returning home from labour work they consume liquor which is mostly purchased from shop and is not prepared at home. Similarly on Sundays or the days on which they take fish or meat, liquor is necessary. The prohibition policy has not largely affected the consumption of liquor. Liquor consumption is also common at the time of rituals and festivals.

Utensils

Earthenware as well as aluminium and brass utensils are used.

Usually Kolams do not burn lamps at night. They keep fire burning in the centre of the hut. During the rains and in winter, members of the family sleep around it. No furniture except a cot is seen in a Kolam hut. Of late, due to development, electricity has reached their villages and some houses have electricity, modern furniture etc.

Dress

The men-folk wear *dhoti*, shirt, *shela* (shoulder cloth), cap and turban, (*Mundasa*). A *Shalu* or *Uparna/Dupatta* is taken on shoulders. This is the traditional dress but is still continued specially by the elderly people. The youths put on pant, shirt or manila shirt etc. While going to weekly market they wear *Dupatta*.

The women traditionally wear *Lugda*, **Didki*, and *Choli* (Kujesam), but young school girls are now putting on saree and (*zampur*) blouse. One end of the *Lugda* drawn over the head drops in Maratha style on right shoulder.

---

* *Didki* : A short 4 meter Lugda worn in a style in which one leg is covered while the other leg is half-covered.

Though the new generation has adopted pant, shirts, saree and blouses, the traditional dress is also used by majority of the elderly people.

Ornaments

The women use ornaments which are mostly made-up of silver. These include Mukkeram (*Mukra*), *Sakli Sari*, Bavatya, Patlya (*Patlikul*), Jodve (*Mattela*) Sikke masrya etc. These are purchased from the market or from the goldsmith by placing order.

The men do not put on ornaments, except a silver bracelet (*kada*) around the wrist, and silver strap (*kardoda*) around waist.

Tattooing

Tattooing is very common on many parts of the body and in women it includes various signs *e.g.* Moon, Sun, Tulsi-Vrindavan, Tree, Gauri, Scorpion, Banyan tree, Bajarangbali, Rama's Chariot, Sita's Bathplace, Chumbal, Rangoli designs, five women carrying milk (Gaulan), some idols of Gods and Goddesses, Sun and Moon etc. Men may have their names tattooed on hands.

Certain symbols indicating the totem of the clan like Tiger, Dog, Goat, Paddy, Ambadi, Kumbha, Sheep, Buffalo, Cow etc. are very common. These are worshipped and may be painted on the walls of the house etc.

The Village and Housing

The villages of the Kolam are usually called '*Pod* ', as it is always an annexe of some other village inhabited by non-Kolams. The *Pod is* well-planned and at the centre there is a *Chavdi*. In front of the *Chavdi* the village Goddess in installed (Gabhuri). Open space is left for conducting meeting etc. around the *Chavdi.* Around the *Chavdi* houses/huts are constructed in rows or circles. Gaon-Bandhani or Fulzadni programmes and the feast, dances on the occasion are celebrated in the open space.

Usually, they construct *kuccha* huts with two rooms and a courtyard. The roof of the hut is either thatched with grass or has country tiles. The houses are not very safe and hence are vulnerable. Their walls are of wooden ribs or of interlaced bamboo strips, plastered with mud and cow dung from the out-side. They have one hut for one household and another one for the cattle.

Spiritual Culture

Religion

Like all other tribals, Kolams are also animists and nature-worshippers. Ancestor-worship is also observed. They have many local Gods and Goddesses which are worshipped on different occasions. Elaborate rituals and festivals are observed. They consider themselves as Hindus and worship many Hindu Gods and particularly the Goddess Renuka of Mahur. Inspite of the advent of Muhammedan religion, or on the background of conversions to Christianity by the Church in the area, there are almost no religious converts in the Kolam in Yavatmal or Chandrapur district. Even in the wave of conversion to Buddhism, there are no converts from the Kolam. Dr. Bhau Mandavkar also confirms this observation.[2]

This fact may be due to their strong belief in their traditional religion, and deities and staunch ethnocentric tendencies. While Gonds are often reluctant to consider their religion as Hindu, Kolam do consider themselves as Hindu. Many customs, traditions and rituals simulate those of the Hindus. Many Kolams consider themselves as having their origin from Pandavas of the Great Mahabharata. However, they also have their Gods and deities which are of typical tribal tradition. Their scheme of social organisation based on God-groups is much similar to the Gonds. The marriage ritual and further customs related to marriage are also similar to the Gonds.

The marriage ritual and customs related to marriage are also similar to the Pardhans in the area. Probably it is due to their Kolam association with the Hindu non-tribals around them, that they attained certain degree of acculturation which resulted in the adoption of non-tribal Hindu practices. They are not considered as impure by Hindus and are permitted to enter Hindu temples.[3]

The Religious Leader

Like all other tribes there is a religious leader who takes initiative in organising religious function and worship. The *Pujari/Bhagat* worships the Gods and the *Ghusadi/Gosai,* Ghatya/Ghatyak also participate in religious ceremonies. Specially in the *Gaon-Bandhani* function *Ghusadi* leads the ritual and the ritual dances which follow.

Tarma cooks the food at the time of such ceremonies. Thus he is a cook for the public functions of the tribe. Ghatya also works as a messenger of the Panchayat in the village. It is observed that the functionaries in this particular tribe are not purely concerned with religious functions but are entrusted with other functions of the Panchayat concerned with the village.

In some returns *Palshil Nayakun* has also been reported as the chief of all these functionaries as he is the oldest person with authority and knows all the traditional details about such functions. He is the senior most Naik who has control even over the panchayat.

The dates and timings of the community ritual are decided by the Naik in consultation with the Panchayat. The Ghatya, Tarma etc. perform the duties with the actual performance of the function under the guidance of the Naik. Thus the religious and the profane duties are grouped together under the general guidance of the Naik and Panchayat.

Gods and Goddesses

The various Gods and Goddesses worshipped include, Aai Devi, Mahurta Devi, Renuka, Karai-Marai, Bhovani, Chandaka, Bhimayak, Bhivsan, Jaitur, Jelayak, San-Surayak, Maroti, Pettadiyam, Bhairum, Mhasoba etc. In every village there is a central temple of the Goddess or of the Pandavas. It may be recalled that the Kolam consider themselves as originating from the race of the Pandavas. In Rajura tehsil, the Goddess *Marai* at Marai Patan is important place of worship of the Kolams.

The important religious ritual reported in the returns are *Gaon Bandhani*, *Bhivsan Anghol* (Bathing of the God Bhivsan). The *Gaon Bandhani* function is usually in May, after the *Pola*. Another functions called *Fulzadni*, *Aaichi Sat*, are also important.

On the Gudi Padwa day the Panchayat of the village is re-elected. They also celebrate *Nag-Panchami*, Pola, Dushera, Diwali and Holi in traditional manner.

Of-late they have adopted the Ganesh festival and Durga festival also.

Bhivsan Anghol is a ceremony when an idol of God Bhivsan prepared out of a tree-trunk is taken out in procession and bathed in water. This is in the Hindu month of Vaishakh or Paush (falls in January).

Once in a year, in Paush *Devichi Sat* ritual is performed on any Tuesday in the month of Paush.

Description of some Gods and Goddesses is given below:

Renuka

Goddess Renuka at Mahur is near the Kolam habitats in Yavatmal district. Many Kolams are devotes of the Goddess. During the *Navaratri* festival around Dushera, Kolams in the area congregate at the temple and sing religious songs and dance, thus worshipping the Goddess. They perform rituals to keep their pledge/vows (*Navas*). Locally, in a Kolam *pod*, a heap of stones may be erected to symbolise this Goddess and *Puja* is offered at that shrine.

Aaya

Aai/Aaya is installed below a Neem tree on the Eastern side of the *Pod.* This Goddess wards off evils and diseases and in case of the spread of epidemics cocks and goats are offered to this Goddess. When the Kolam men worship God Bhimayak, the women worship the Goddess.

Karai-Marai is a Goddess which protects the borders of the village.

Bhimayak

Bhimayak usually *Bhima* or *Bhivsan* (*ayak* means God) is an important deity of the Kolam. It is usually installed on the Western side of the village under a Mahua tree. Before the sowing of seeds, they are ceremonially offered to the God to seek his blessings for a good harvest season. This ritual is called *Baibaki* which is preferably performed on a Wednesday. A ritual concerned with this God is *Bhivsan Anghol* (Bathing of God Bhivsan). The *Fulzadni* ritual is also performed near this God.

Jaitur

Jaitur is an important and respected God. It is usually installed under Tembhurni or Maharukh (*Pipple*) trees. It is at some places which is away from the humdrum of the town *i.e.* some lonely place. A wild-pig is sacrificed before this God. Before the Hindu month of Shravan or after that month, this sacrifice is offered. Women are tabooed from visiting this shrine with a black *Lugda/Saree* as it offends this God.

Pettadiyam

On the four corners of the village there are four Gods. On the North-East corner is the Pettadiyam. The *Gaon-Bandhani* ritual starts from this corner which is called *Mudal* corner.

Magic

The Kolam believe in magic. There are persons who practise magic and black-magic also. Mostly it is used against the enemy either for killing him or for ruining him. *Mantras* are used for snake bites and scorpion bites, and they believe that it helps in removing the poison. Even for dog bites *mantras* are used. Some have reported that the *mantras* are used for giving relief for minor injuries on the body.

Rituals and Festivals

There are many rituals and festivals which are celebrated by the Kolam. These are as follows:

Rituals

1. *Sati* or *Gaon-Bandhani*
2. Korod or Phanmondi
3. Burri
4. Mohdombari
5. Churaghali or Matya
6. Chait
7. *Bai-Baki*
8. Bhimayak/Bhivsan Anghol
9. Jaitur *Pooja*
10. Waghai *Pooja*
11. Morang Dev *Pooja*

Festivals

1. Fulzadni or Zadperni
2. Kargul
3. Nag Panchami
4. Pola
5. Atari
6. Akharpakha
7. Dushera

8. Diwali
9. Holi
10. Metti-Diyam
11. Pettadiyam
12. Aaichi Pooja/*Aaichi Sat*

A few of these rituals and festivals are described below.

Gaon-Bandhani

This is an important ritual which is called *Sati* in Kolami dialect. For the Kolam-*Pod* this ritual is a festive occasion and none tries to miss it. Gaon Bandhani literally means fortification of the village boundary so as to ward-off all evils including ghost, out-side Gods, epidemics, diseases etc. If the *Pod* is new this may be celebrated after three years. All the Kolams assemble in their *Chavdi*, where the Panchayat meeting is held. The Naik discusses the dates with the people and some day is fixed. Usually, from the Hindu month of Vaishakha up to full-moon day in Jeshtha, it may be celebrated. Thus, it falls some where in May or June.

A Bhagat or *Ghusadi* may be called, if necessary, from another Kolam village. Contributions are collected from the villagers in cash or in kind. The function lasts for two days. The Chief-Goddess in the locality is first worshipped at the hands of the Naik. A goat and a cock are sacrificed before the Goddess. This Goddess is mostly in front of the Chavdi which is the centre of the village. Sacred fire is then kindled in front of the Chavdi.

The actual Gaon Bandhani ritual starts in the evening by the time of sun-set. On the four corners of the village the Kolam have four Gods. On the North-East corner is God *Pettadiyam* and this corner is called Mudal-Kon. After offering worship to the God, a plough is fixed in the Earth and the *Bandhan* commences. Three stones are placed and at the centre a wooden plug is fixed. Below the stone and the plug a cock and a chicken are buried. The *Pujari* from the village performs the *Pooja* and then using the arrow-head of a spear, he starts pulling a line on the boundary of the village till it reaches the North-West corner of the village which is called *Mahadev-Kon.*

The same process is repeated and the line drawn towards South-West corner which is called *Moran-Kon*. God *Moran* is important because, while settling at a new place and establishing the village, *Moran* is the first God which is installed and worshipped. Again the same *pooja* is offered and plugs are fixed. Then the line is drawn further to South-East corner which is called *Satvan-Kon*. Here also similar ritual is performed. Later, the line is drawn again to reach the starting point *i.e. Mudal-Kon* on the North-East. But a small entry point is left. Here also a plough and a plug are fixed between three stones and *pooja* and sacrifices are offered.

While this ritual is in progress a few Kolams from the village follow the *Bhagat* and sprinkle the sacrificial blood from within and outside of the line, while one person goes on putting salt and sand on the line which is being drawn. At the end the *Bhagat* stands on the stone of the *Mudal-Kon* and invokes and invites the Goddess of Mahur to come and protect the village. After this the *Bhagat* inspects the line to the tunes of the *daf* and flute which are being played loudly. No Kolam can go out till the whole ritual is over. Similarly, no outsider is allowed to enter during the ritual and if he enters he is penalised. The Kolams in the village eat, drink and dance throughout the night.

Moha Dombari

In Kolami dialect this ritual is called *Burri*. The mahua tree (*Madhuca indica*) and flowers are important in this ritual and hence the name. Some Kolams perform this ritual on the Gudi Padwa day along with Phanmodi.

For this festival about two *paylee* (about 1 kg.) dried mahua flowers are collected in advance. Contributions from each house are also collected which may be equal to one *anna* (about ten paise) and quarter kilo *charoli* (*chironji*). On the previous day of the festival the following verse is happily sung by the people to express their joy.

Savadi boddet and keri
Tolline Bhurri Anada

Why is this hum drum in the courtyard of the *Chavdi*?
Tomorrow we will celebrate Moha dombari.

On the Tij (Akshayya Tritiya) the Moha dombari is celebrated and the men folk go to the forest for hunting. The women are not permitted to put on *kajal* or *kunku* because that may bring bad omen. In the evening they return with the animals killed in the hunt and these are cooked near the *Chavdi* throughout the night. They eat and dance to the tune of music. Mahua liquor and charoli is consumed but all these things are first offered to the Goddess and then eaten by all.

Phan Modi

On the Hindu new year day which is called *Varsha Pratipada* or Gudi Padwa, they celebrate *Phan Modi*. Ploughing of the farms is to be started as the old harvest has been taken out, so as to clear the remaining stalks of the jawar or other saplings, the Kolams observe this ritual. Mahajan, who is the Vice-President of the Caste Panchayat gets the honour as the Kolams start this work from his farm. The dried stalks are collected at one place in the farm and are burnt. That fire is worshipped and all this is completed before sunrise.

On the same *i.e. Varsha Pratipada* day the Kolam worship the Goddess and make a symbolic and ceremonial beginning by curious method. One egg of a hen is wrapped in a cloth and held in suspension before the Goddess. The Kolams stand with hunting sticks in their hands while the Ghatya shouts calling the name of each animal.

"Sasha *S S S* la *S S S*
and other shout
Aala Aala *S S S*

and while uttering this they beat the egg with the stick. This procedure is continued by calling the names of other animals like deer, wild pig etc. It is believed by them that this will give them success in hunting.

Fulzadni/Zadperni

After the leguminous plants grow, these festivals are celebrated. After the first showers of rain the plants and creepers start growing and bear flowers. Once the flower starts getting fruits the flowers wither. This is called Fulzadni. Hence this festival is celebrated at that stage. Later the fruit starts developing seeds seed which is the basis for sowing the new plant. Hence this stage is celebrated as *Zadperni* (sowing of the plant).

This festival is for two days. On the previous day, boys go to jungle and pluck leaves of teak tree. On the *Zadperni* day is the beginning of plucking of teak leaves which is never done during rainy season. These leaves are worshiped and honoured on the *Zadperni* day. The leaves are distributed in the village and the villagers attach the leaves to the roof doors, grain reservoir, compound etc. The remaining leaves are kept near the place of Goddess which is in front of the *Chavdi.* If some house is omitted from distribution of leaves it is considered as an insult and that point is raised in the Panchayat on the next day. The Ghatya has to apologise on behalf of the Panchayat.

At night the Kolams may adopt a typical procedure for fun making. A few Kolams may go to some one's house and start digging his courtyard. If the people are awaken they stop digging and the house owner has to serve milk to them by way of honouring them. But if he doesn't awake the whole of the courtyard is dug off. The whole episode is a warning to the person that at night he must already be alert.

The next day is the main festival day. They bring corn, cucumber, ladies finger, *Valuk* etc. from the farms and some flowers. They collectively worship all their Gods on the boundary of the villages and offer these vegetables etc. This is offering of the new produce to the God. A goat is sacrificed in front of the God Bhimayak and pieces of his flesh are distributed in all houses of the village.

In the evening they prepare *chapatti* from wheat or jowar floor and the panchas hide one *chapatti* under the teak leaves kept near the Bhimayak. Then all the Kolam women are asked to find out the *chapatti.* While they are in search of *chapatti* they come along with their meals served in the teak leaves, so that if they are unable to find out the *chapatti* quickly they can take their meals and start the search. If they locate the *chapatti* all of them eat it and if they are unable to find out they have to return home and bring one *chapatti* from each house as a penalty. Thus the Kolam women are associated with this festival and add to the fun fair and merry-making at night. The people kindle a bon-fire in front of the *Chavdi* and sing songs which mean that all the harmful insects, flies etc. may be burnt in the fire. There is a lot of singing, dancing and drinking of liquor.

REFERENCES

1. Karve, Iravati, *Marathi Lokanchi Sanskrit*, R.J. Deshmukh & Co. 1962 (2nd Ed.) Pune, p 130
2. Gazetteer of India, *Chandrapur District Gazetteer* Maharashtra State, 2nd Revised Edition 1973, p. 437
3. Mandaokar, Bhau, *Kolam*, Seva Prakashan, Amravati, 1966 p. 162

3

LIFE CYCLE RITUALS

Birth

The Kolam believe in re-birth. They say that birth depends upon the good deeds in previous life. *Suin* (midwife) is called for the delivery who is a local lady traditionally experienced in the job.

Impurity is observed after the birth of the child for 45 days. However, some reported this period as 15 days while others as 30 days.

Name giving ceremony is observed on the 5th day from the birth of the child. Five auspicious lamps made of wheat flour and oil are burnt and are called *Dnyandeep* (lamps of knowledge) and *Til-Gul* (sesamum seeds and jaggery) are distributed. Feast is given to all Kolams from the village. This may be done even on the 12th day and called *Barsa.*

Name for the child is selected by the elderly person, usually the grand-father and grand-mother of the child. Names are given after the fore-fathers. (If grand-father is dead – his name is also given.) Names of Gods and Goddess are also given, for example, Bhima (after God Bhimayak), Waghu (after the God Waghoba etc.).

Head shaving is done any time but usually after 2 to 4 months. A ceremony called *Kudmul* is observed while shaving the head.

Puberty

When a girl attains puberty a ceremony is observed. Elderly women perform the *Oti i.e.* they put wheat, coconut and other auspicious things in the pouch of the girl. A worm (*ali*) is broken on the door in name of that girl. After three days of impurity, the old women eat *Kumli* (sesamum seeds and jaggery) and feast is given to them. About fifteen old women are given 5-6 *paylees* (about 7-8 kilos) of grain and a cock which they eat outside the village. Killing of the worm sounds symbolic as it simulates menstruation.

Marriage

Though the Kolams have no sub-tribes they are divided into number of exogamous groups (phratries) for the purpose of marriage. Marriage between members of the same groups is forbidden. Thus they have endogamy at tribe level and exogamy at clan level. Similarly, a man is not allowed to marry two sisters. Marriages are adult marriages, and child marriage is not seen. During the Hindu month Poush, neither the betrothal nor marriage can take place, as this month is fixed for ancestor worship. If a marriage is not performed after betrothal, a fine in cash is imposed on the party which breaks the contract. Usually it ranges between five to ten rupees and may go up to hundred rupees. According to their tradition, the tribe or the women from the tribe used to capture husbands and even today this persists in different forms. If it is not possible to find a match for the son, the boy, along with his friends goes to the jungle where the girl may be working with her friends or relatives. The boy has to go and persuade the girl to catch his hand and the girl's party tries to beat him and make him run away. If he fights and succeeds in catching hold of the girl who is protected by her girl friends, he can officially claim her as his wife. Later on, the marriage is performed after the boy pays bride-price of a few rupees to the girl's father. Of late, this procedure has lost its originality but still remains in a token form, and is just a pretence which is arranged before hand.

Forms of Marriage

Various Forms of Marriage

1. Marriage by capture is practiced. It may be both, factual and symbolic. But of late it is only symbolic.
2. Marriage by trial is not in vogue.
3. Marriage by purchase is also not practised.
4. Marriage by service is present. Bride-groom who is unable to pay the bride-price has to stay at his father-in-law's place and serve for one year or so to compensate the bride-price.
5. Marriage by mutual consent is present.
6. Marriage by elopement is present.
7. Marriage by intrusion is also present. A girl may enter the

house of a boy and insist or marriage. Marriage by compulsion is not common, it is rare.

8. Marriage by negotiations in which negotiations are conducted by the parents, is present.
9. Marriage by courtship (love marriage) is also present.

Marriage by exchange is seen particularly between the daughter of the brother and the son of the sister. This is also termed as *Sat-lot* marriage. At times sister's daughter may also be married to brother's son in the *Sat-lot* marriage.

The age of marriage for the girls ranges between fifteen to eighteen and for the boys between eighteen to twenty one years of age. The marriages are settled by the traditional Panchayat of the Kolam-*Pod.* A meeting is held either in the morning or in the evening in the open space of the *Chavdi* for this purpose. The custom of bride-price is still in vogue. It ranges from Rs. 100 in cash to Rs. 300 and one quintal jawar and may vary according to the negotiations. According to some, the jawar or the amount may be increased so that it may suffice for giving meals to the whole village. A fixed sum of Rs. 7 is paid to the village Panchayat and is called *Pado*. The marriage ceremony takes place at the bridegrooms' place.

The marriage ceremony is performed at the bride's place, when the groom is unable to pay the bride-price as he has to serve at the father-in-law's place for one year or till the amount is repaid. In all other cases the marriage is performed at the bride-groom's place.

Bigamy is practised though it is rare these days, and in such cases there may be two wives.

The Ritual

The Marriage Pendal (Mandap)

The pendal is of either nine or of twelve pillars (Deri) which ought to be of *Salai* or different trees; but the central pillar around which the marriage is solemnised (Mund) must necessarily be of *Salai* (Bosvellia serrata) tree. Other pillars may be from the trunks of other trees like Mahua, Umbar etc. The roof of the pendal (*Mandap*) is covered by branches and leaves of Jamun tree. The bride and the groom are seated in between two Munds.

The ritual includes applying turmeric-power to the bride and the groom, bathing, worship of Gods and pouring of water at the time of solemnising the marriage. Water is poured thrice on the head of the bride-groom and twice over the head of the bride. There is no ritual of touching of the bride's toe to the groom's toe (which is common among the Gonds). Of late, some Kolam also add the rituals from the surrounding non-tribal communities.

At the marriage ceremony the God's worshipped include Amma diyyam, Matayak, *Aai* (Mother Goddess), *Devi* (Goddess) and the forefathers. Some have also mentioned Bhivsan, Atmak, Jaitur, Silatad, Bhimayak – Diyyam and other local or domestic or clan Gods and Goddesses; Marampili, Mesai, Bhutai etc.

A feast is given to the whole village community and liquor is also served. Dancing and singing follows the feast. Of late, the nature of feast has changed and consumption of liquor is also reduced.

Divorce

Traditionally divorce can be obtained. Either of the spouses can demand divorce. For that purpose wife or husband – any one of them can approach the traditional Panchayat of the village. The grounds on which divorce may be obtained are given below :

1. If there are quarrels between the husband and wife and they are unable to put up with each other.
2. Impotency.
3. Infidelity of either of the spouses leading to illegal sex relations with other persons.
4. If the wife is unable to bare child-bareness.
5. If either of them is suffering from veneral diseases.
6. If they don't like each other.
7. If the girl is getting cruel treatment from her father-in-law or mother-in-law.

In all such cases the aggrieved party may approach the Panchayat and put his/her case before the Panchayat. The Panchayat takes the decision and grants divorce. Fines are also imposed usually on the person who demands divorce, but, fine may be imposed on both of them. The fine imposed is to be deposited with the Panchayat, or, the person who is obtaining divorce has to pay it to the other party. This is in fact the returning of the bride price when the girl obtains the divorce.

Re-marriage

A divorced man or woman is permitted to re-marry with other person. In some cases re-marriage with the younger brother of the husband is also allowed. Even a widow may marry her husband's younger brother. This is similar to the custom in the Gonds where marriage of a woman with husband's younger brother is permitted.

The Gond tradition seems to have been adopted even in the Kolam tribals. Marriage with the elder brother of the husband is tabooed. One of the reasons is the high respect which is given to the elder brother and the other reason is that the elderly woman prefers marriage with the younger brother. When the marriage is with other persons who may be related or not, it should be out-side the gotra *i.e.* in another God-group.

Marriages are permitted in certain relations, *e.g.* brother's daughter may be married to sister's son or this may be on a reciprocal basis (*Sat-lot*).

Family

The Kolam family is patrilocal.

Traditionally they have cellular families because after marriage of the sons they separate from parents family within two to three years. However, the surname of the father continues.

Inheritance is patrilineal and only the son gets share in the property. If there is no son, the daughter may get it. In case of conflict the Panchayat settles the dispute.

Usually, the head of the family is male but in case there is no male member, the senior female member may also function as the head of the family. The position of the woman in the house is not of a subordinate but is very important. Except in religious matter she is consulted in taking all the important decisions of the house including settling of marriages, incurring of expenditure, and all other matters. In one return she was described as, "Home Minister". If she is not given due importance she may ask for divorce. Women do all the domestic work, maintain the house, do cooking, milking of the cattle and also go to farm as labourers, bring fire-wood from the forest and do all other necessary jobs. She participates in social activities of village. Women have blind faith and believe in all customs and traditions. They are adverse to family planning but of late, are accepting the programme. On the whole, women hold very important position in the family.

1. Naik, Ghatya, Karbhari in Kolam *Chavdi* at Pijdura

2. A view of Kolam *Chavdi* at Pijdura

3. Kolam huts.

4. Advocate Leena Deogaonkar discussing with office-bearers of Kolam Panchayat at Mangli *Pod*

5. Kolams discussing their local problems with Advocate Leena

6. Kolam *Pod* at Pijdura Kolam children near their huts.

7. Shri Masram and his family at Kolam Pod at Mangli

8. Kolams trom two Pods assembled at Pijdura.
(At extreme right in front row is Shriram Zode, the first B.A., B.Ed. youth from Kolams).

Death

Like other tribal populations in the area, the Kolam bury the dead. They believe in re-birth and have a belief that the soul takes birth in a new body. Thus forefathers return by rebirth.

The death impurity is observed for 2-3 hours, *i.e.* till the dead body is removed from the village and is buried. All activities in the village including household work is stopped till this is done. In a few returns the period of impurity was stated as one month. Urine of cow (*Gomutra*) is sprinkled as a purifier.

On the third day a function called *Bonam* is observed which is similar to the *Tervi* observed in the non-tribals in the surrounding area. Rice equal to eight *paylees* (about 12 kilos) is cooked and a hen (if the dead person is a woman) or a cock (if the dead person is a man) is killed by forcefully dashing its head on the spot. Then it is cooked. Juar flour is also cooked (Kanya) and two plates with these edibles are served to an old woman and an old man. Others sit around and call the soul of the dead person. It is believed that the soul enters the body of some persons present there.

For the peace to the departed soul a ritual called Gondhal is performed within 1-2 or 3 years. Persons from the same sept or clan participate. Idols or carvings are prepared which are of gold, silver or from the wood of *Char* tree. This represents the dead person. This is called *Ghadvine*. On the outskirts of the village, on the banks of a river or lake this function which simulates the *shraddha* is performed. Preferably, it is performed on a Monday in the Hindu month of Shravan or Paush or on any Monday in January. The head of the son of the dead person is shaved which is called *Vapan*. Before this shaving, the head of a cock is buried and the soil from that place is carried to the river, lake etc., where the head-shaving of the son is done. A goat is also sacrificed. In a few returns this function was reported to be performed after a month.

4

KOLAM FOLK-LORE

Language

The Kolam speak a dialect which is classified as a Dravidian language. It has no script. Irawati Karve also calls it a Dravidian language. G.A. Grierson has shown that it has some primary forms of the Telugu and Kannada languages, and further opines that Kolami simulates Gondi dialect.[1]

The Kolami Dialect

Their dialect is called Kolami dialect. It is closely related to Gondi. In some aspects it resembles Telugu while some characteristics resemble Canarese *i.e.* the Kannada. However, it differs from the Gondi spoken by the Gonds in the neighbourhood. G.A. Grierson points to its analogy with the Toda dialect of the Nilgiris and opines that philologically Kolams, "be considered as remnant of the Dravidian tribe who have not been involved in the development of the principal Dravidian languages or of a tribe who have not originally spoken a Dravidian form of speech."[2] Grierson also states that the Kolami from Berar (now Vidarbha region of Maharashtra State) agrees in so many particulars with the Bhili spoken in the Pusad taluka of Bashim (Washim) and the Naik of Chanda (Chandrapur) that they can almost be considered as one and the same dialect. Hiralal has also suggested that the Kolam may be connected with the Kolas, a tribe akin to the Todas who consider the Kollamalai Hills as their original home. Russel and Hiralal, basing their view on Grierson's analogy of Kolami with the Naiki (of Naik Gonds) from Chanda (Chandrapur), and further stating that the head of the Kolam village (*Pod*) is called a Naik, suggest that the Kolams may be connected with the Naik Gonds (from Chandrapur).[3]

Dr. M.B. Emenue has also described Kolami as a Dravidian

language. Dr. Setu Madhav Rao Pagdi, Dr. Irawati Karve have also supported this view.

Dr. Bhau Mandaokar opines that in Kolami, roots of many words from Tamil, Telugu, Malayalam and Kannada languages are found and as such he hints that Kolami could be the aboriginal dialect which contains the original roots of these four Dravidian languages.[4] Here he comes closer to the statement made by Grierson when he calls Kolami as a primordial form of the Telugu and Kannada languages. In the Kolami spoken by the Kolams from Yavatmal and Chandrapur districts many Marathi words have been adopted and find a place in their dialect.

Dr. Mandaokar agrees with Russell and Hiralal when he states that the Naiki of Chandrapur and Kolami are much similar and opines that Naik (Gonds) and Kolam are the same. However, so far as similarity in the Bhili of Bhils (Pusad) is concerned he opines that the Kolami dialect was wrongly recorded as Bhili during census and hence it is not but Bhili Kolami itself.[5]

Colonel Mackenzie is of the view that "all their songs and ballads and borrowed from the Marathas, even their workmen when girding corn sing Marathi songs." Even Dr. Emenue, Russell and Hiralal have expressed similar views, but Dr. Bhau Mandaokar has contradicted this view. He states that 'the Kolams living in forest and on hills are very shy and being unable to converse freely in Marathi are reluctant to communicate and, hence the researchers could not communicate and collect their songs. However, the Kolams do have their own Kolami songs, even though due to the surrounding Marathi influence, 25 per cent Marathi words have entered in their songs.[6]

Dr. Emenue has listed 1075 Kolami words while Dr. Setu Madhav Pagdi about 1800 words. The original Kolami words are very difficult to pronounce but many of them have undergone changes and come closer to the counterpart in Marathi language, in particular from the *Varadhi* dialect. For example, he has cited the example of the word *pabuj* from Kolami which means an old man, however, the Kolams living near towns used the word *Buddiyak* which comes from the Marathi word *Budha* popularly used in the four districts of Varahad (Amravati, Akola, Yavatmal and Buldhana). Dr. Mandaokar claims to have collected 500 new words which trace back to original Kolami dialect.[7] Many Gondi words are found in the present Kolami which is very natural because they have the same ethnic origin.

Folk-Songs

Like many other tribal communities, the Kolam also have folk-literature. They have traditional folk-songs which are sung on occasions. These may be broadly classified as per the themes or occasions on which they are sung.

A few songs are given below:

Ritual Songs

While worshipping deities, songs in praise of Gods and Goddesses are sung which can be classified as *Pooja* (worship) songs.

A Pooja Song

Rena Rena Re Rena, Rena Rena Re
Ura Devi Ennive Devi
Inung Narel – Shendur
Ura Bhimayak Ennive Bhimayak,
Inung Pillu Pichuk
Ura Jaitur Ennive Jaitur
Inung Tuke Urmakad
Ura Maroti Ennive Maroti
Inung Beli Phutane
Ura Marayak Ennive Marayak
Inung Nalapuliye

This is a song for performing the *Pooja* of Gods and Goddesses. O Goddesses you are our mother and we are your children. We offer a coconut and *sindur* to you. You bless us.

O God Bhimayak we offer a chicken to you.
O God Jaitur we offer the dish which you like very much.
O God Maroti we offer jaggery and fried grams to you.
O God Marayak we offer the vegetable which you like most.
O God bless us all.

Another Pooja Songs

Re Rena Re Rena

Indi Yena diyalakung diyal Yena Watev
Bara Meyane tav Yerd Tanat Wattev
Diyalung Yena Shendur, Bukka, Siyyur
Ral Gi, Kisilttna Kapur Yena Siyyur
Soni ani Paiku Sukhi Dukhanet Vettorur yeta
Yendet Iyyeltad Pik-Pani Yenang aod Yena
Podilav Sebbungsathi Taned lagave Yena
Muttung Yendug Ovval Yedad Payajen Yena

This song is in praise of God.

O God you come and bless us throughout twelve months. We offer you *Shendur, Bukka, Siyyur, Ral* and ignite *Kapur.* We also offer you money and all other things. You give us happiness and take away our pains. Let our crops grow well.

This song is sung at the time of the worship of traditional Gods.

Pooja Song

Oora Devi song

Rena Rena Re Rena, Rena Rena Re
Ware Ware Oara Devi
Aame Watume Alange
Aame Watume Alange
Kal Kiyya Sukhame Apeye

Ware Ware Bhimayak Diyyam
Ware Ware Bhimayak Diyyam
Aame Watume Alange
Aame Watume Sukhame Apeye

Ware Ware Jaitur Diyyam
Aame Watume Alange, Jaitur
Kal Kiyya Sukhame Apeye

Ware Ware Amma Diyyam
Aame Watume Alange
Aame Watume Amma Diyyam
Kal Kiyya Sukhaya Apeye

The tribal people worship the Moon, the Sun and other things from nature.

"Oh, Goddess Oora Devi, we have come to you, please bless us.
"Oh, God Bhimayak you please bless us.
Oh, God Jaitur please come and bless us.
Oh, Goddess "Aamma" you please come and bless us.

We all are like your children so forgive our mistakes.
This song is also in praise of clan Gods like Ghettalal, Pikkalal etc.

Rena Rena Re Rena Re
Annete Marge Ghettalal Pejite
Ghettalal Pejite
Annete Marge Pikkalal Pejite
Pikkalal Pejite
Annete Marge Tongenal Pejite
Tongenal Pejite
Annete Marge Tikanenal Pejite
Tikanenal Pejite
Annete Marge Arulinal Pejite
Arulinal Pejite
Annete Marge Tallal Pejite
Tallal Pejite
Annete Marge Susulinal Pejite
Susulinal Pejite

Oh, God Ghettalal we offer you *Pooja* so that you will pardon us for our mistakes. Some of us have ailments in body. Some have problems with knees or legs. Some have fever while others suffer from headache or bodyache. Some have lost their parents while some have lost their children. Some are about to die. This means that all have committed mistakes. So we are worshipping god Pikkalal Tongenal Arulinal, Tallal and Susulinal.

The function of *Gaon-Bandhani* is an important ritual. The village is fortified against all evil things and bad omen by this ritual. The following songs are sung during this ritual.

In praise of the Goddess at *Mahur* :

Mahurta Devi Tandung Wattina
Tandung Toda ?
Bara Menela Punja
Tineng Wattin ! (1)

Mahurta Palegama Tandung Wattina
Tandung Toda ?
Bara Menela Punja
Tineng Wattin ! (2)
Mahurta Palegama Uddeng Suleng Tang
Anang Ka (k) Da Tang Toda ?
Bara Menela Khushi
Kakeng Battin ! (3)

Aaura Pillakul Iyura Pillakul
Tadung Kultera Tadung Toda ?
Satti Oleng Wattev:

Meaning

O Mahur Goddess why have you come ? And for what have you not come ?

For accepting twelve months Puja !

O Palegama from Mahur why have you come ?

For accepting twelve months Puja !

O Palegama from Mahur

Why are you standing up and sitting down ?

For enjoying the happiness pleasure for twelve months. Women and girls from that town and children from out town have come together, for what purpose?

To see the ceremony of *"Gaon Bandhani"* !

A jocular song on *Gaon Bandhani* ritual :

Nevali Bhete Kave Miyada
Taneda Miyada Taneda Toda ?
Supari Save Seddina
Miya Tiragad Yenar !

Meaning

The tortoise is grazing on the banks of river. We do not know as to, on what it is grazing.
The Bhagat's belly has gone down, hence, they say, he is grazing.

A festival called *Kargul* is celebrated on the *Nag Panchami* day. This song is sung on the occasion.

Kargul song

Shili Modal, Moduk Modal
Aare Rama Raghoba Re !
Teke Modal, Madgi Modal ! Aareo
Sitta Modal, Meli Modal ! Aareo
Renga Modal, Burra Modal ! Aareo

Like this the song may be continued by adding the names of various trees and ending by 'Aare Rama Raghoba Re'.

Davandi song (Announcement song)

Before the *Gaon Bandhani* ritual the *Panchas* announce the forthcoming ritual and contributions are invited for which this song is sung.

Savadi Boddeta Tand Keriye
Ye Deva Lala !
Savadi Boddeta Tand Keriye
Ye Nekun Ban
Ren Sandal Pan Yenar !
Savadi Boddet Tand Keriye
Ye Deva Lala !
Savadi Boddet Tand Keriye

Ye Nekun Ban
Sire Biyam Yenar ! (2)

Savadi Boddet Tand Keriye
Ye Deva Lala !
Savadi Boddet Tand Keriye
Ye Nekun Ban
Muttela Pokkela Yenar ! (3)

Savadi Boddet Tand Keriye
Ye Deva Lala !
Savadi Boddet Tand Keriye
Ye Nekum Ban
Chittel Bhashi Sesa Yenar ! (4)

Meaning

What is the humdrum in the premises of the Chavdi ? O my God !

What is the humdrum in the premises of the Chavdi ?
-O Naik Baba !
They say contribute one Anna (six paise)
What is the humdrum in the premises of the Chavdi ?

-O Naik Baba !
they say contribute charoli (chironji)
What is the humdrum…?

-O my God !
They say contribute one paily *Moha*
What is the humdrum…?

-O my God !
What is the humdrum…?

-O Naik Baba !
They say give one unit of salt.

Fulzadni or *Zadperni Song*

A ritual called *Fulzadni* or *Zadperni* is performed to ward off the germs and insects of the adjoining forest from the village. Drums are beaten and flute is played to give music to these songs.

Guchchu Dome

Bhambode Nenjeng Kak Ten Neev
Tang Kaketeev, Guchchu Dome
Purrel Nenjeng Kak Ten Neev
Tang Kaketeev, Guchchu Dome

You were to cook vegetable of big ants, why did you not prepare ?

Oh (God), take away mosquitoes, insects etc. You were to cook vegetable of insects, why did you not prepare?
Oh (God) take away mosquitoes, insects etc.

This song may be continued by repeating the lines and changing the names of insects, flies etc.

Hari – Ramanet Puvva

This is a devotional song, and has a spiritual message.

Jalmeng Wattna Jame
Kur Kakner Yena Bhul
Inneti Kiyyat Shobilad
Hari – Ramaknet Puvva
Hanumannet Ani Shriram net
Okkodiya Bhakti
Andadi Jalarung Mahiti Naval tote Atti
Vela Ani Murkha, Serembipe Yena Poyye
Gurubak Ani Dnyaneshwara Sumttak Toteraware
Tuka Ani Chokhak Ivrun Visarlitam Yend
Galdi Yena olure, Avaret Tatvadnyan Bhulilad yend

Meaning

As you have come to this earth as human beings, try to utter the pious names of lord Shriram – Krishna – Hari. Do not forget these words. Remember the good deeds of these great men and try to do something good.

Shriram and Hanuman are one and the same thing because Hanuman is not complete without Shriram and Shriram is not complete without Seeta. Hence don't get confused.

Though the people know this, they behave foolishly and displease the God.

Saints like Garoba and Dnyaneshwar told this very truth. Saint Tukaram and Chokhoba also told this truth through their *Abhangas* but people forget their teachings.

Marriage Songs

During the marriage ceremony the bride's party and the groom's party cut jokes with each other. For example this song.

Amme Pilla Kandkad

Amme Pilla Kandkad, Amme Pilla Kandkad
Mograknet Puvvakisha, Puvvabarabar Kandkad
Imme Bala Kandkan, Imme Bala Kandkan
Shikuknet Khutekisha, Khutbarabar – Kandkan
Amme Pilla Kandkad, Amme Pilla Kandkad.

Kavarene Ruikishya, Sevveke Ruyyi Yena Kandkad
Imme Bala Kandkan, Imme Bala Kandkan
Mulolite Muloli Gini, Khubi dayyul Kandkan
Amme Pillane Mungalal, Amme Pillane Mungalal
Koya, Koya Mungalal, Yenang Shobhittana Kandkan.

Imme Balane Mungalal, Imme Balane Mungalal
Ir Unakad Habshikisha, Habshilang Kandkad
Amme Pilla Kandkad, Amme Pilla Kandkad
Lakshmi Ani Durga Devilang Kandkad

Imme Lala Kandkan, Imme Lala Kandkan
Mahabharat ta Bhimkisha, Bhimbarabar Kandkan.
Husbar te Hushar gini Ovvol Oleng Kandkad
Gebbuk te Gebbuk gini, Oleng Kandkan
Imme Bala Kandkan, Imme Bala Kandkan.

The bride's parents are praising the girl and at the same time teasing the bridegroom. Our girl is like the delicate flower of *Mogra* and the fragrance of her youth is attracting all. While your son is like the straight trunk of a *Khair* tree and is hard like a soldier.

The girl is fair and looks white like cotton while your boy looks like skeleton and is black in colour.

The nose of our daughter is just becoming to her face while your son's nose is like the handle of a water pump.

Our daughter looks like Laxmi or Goddess Durga, while your so on looks like Balbhima from Mahabharat that means he is ugly.

Our daughter is not only beautiful but also useful for domestic work. As compared to her, your son is a dullard and of low qualities.

The following songs are sung at the time of the culmination of marriage ceremony, when the ritual thread (*Kankan*) on the wrist is taken out.

The Kankan Song I

Usurka Poroka
Aam Babu Parakan

Aam Babu Olane
Kaknyal Sasyure

The leaves of Amla tree, our babu walks by rubbing his stomach.
Our babu is looking, take out the thread from his wrist.

The Kankan Song II

Dada, Aam Dada Olatun
Kaknya Saso
Doi, Aam Doi Olatun
Kaknya Saso

We look at our Dada,
He should take out our thread,
We look at our grand mother,
She should take out our thread.

This song is about the promise given by a husband to his newly married wife about purchasing ornaments etc.

Inne Jamungsathi Kerje Pusadatun
Wattette Katun, Jamung Siyyatun
Tandung Ararativ Buku Kandala Irun Motatun
Inne Jamungsathi Kerje Pusadatun
Angadi Setna Jeritad Sadi Sumdatun
Angadi Setna Reshimatad Zampor Sumdatun

Inne Jamungsathi Kerje Pusadatun
Angadi Setna Saneta Mukkeram Sumdatun
Inne Jamungsathi Kerje Pusadatun
Angadi Setna Chanditav Mattel Sumdatun

Inne Jamungsathi Kerje Pusadatun
Angadi Setna Petlikul Sumdatun
Inne Jamungsathi Kerje Pusadatun
Angadi Setna Tordyal Sumdatun

Inne Jamungsathi Kerje Pusadatun
Sonnarinang Setna Sonetav Gajul Sumdatun
Inne Jamungsathi Kerje Pusadatun

Angadi Setna Kopata Gejra Summatun
Inne Jamungsathi Kerje Pusdatun
Kerje Siyyete Gahan Anatun
Wattel te Katun Jamung Sioyyatun
Tandung Ararative Buku Kandla Irun Matatun

The husband says that he is ready to do anything for the wife. He says, "I shall take loan for you and do anything, even sacrifice my life but please don't weep."

"I shall take a loan from Pusad and purchase a *Jari* saree, a blouse of silk, a golden mukra (a nose ornament)".

The husband again tells her that he will take a loan at Pusad and purchase silver ornaments for her legs, leg fingers, and golden bangles for her. He promises to bring flowers for her. He says that if he is unable to get a loan he may even mortgage himself for the loan and fulfill her desires, but she should stop weeping.

Social as well as family relationships are depicted in some songs. Different topics are covered.

Husband-Wife Relationship

Rena Re Rena Rena Rena Re
Bata Undeve Bai tav Wattine
Tav Wattin te Dada Ghenna Galeve
Ghenna Gholta Gholta Khatyak Tiktene
Khatyak Tiktentena, Kolama Renderal Eddine

Bata Undeve Bayyi Galli Lepeve
Galli Leptive te tav Wattine
Tav Wattine te Dada Ghenna Goleve
Ghenna Golta Golta Khatyak Tiktene
Khatyak Tiktente, Kolama Renderal Yeddine

Bata Undeve Bayyi Kolwal Leyapeve
Kolwal Leptive te Bayyi tav Wattine
Tav Wattin te Dada Ghenna Golve
Ghenna Golta Golta Khatyak Tiktene
Khatyak Tikente, Kolam Renderal Eddin

This song depicts the relationship between Kolam husband and wife. The husband says to the wife that they should live together and respect each others sentiment. They must respect each other and carry on the family life peacefully.

India Pillakul

Indita Pillakul Yenave Magvanung
Ichyute servel Ir Kotva Yendung
Masal Kurtin Karbharal
Magvan Kurten Darbarung
Indita Pillakul Yenave Magvanung
Moppel Sivval Kottva Yedung
Masal Kurtin Karbharal
Magvan Kurten Kam Kakeng
Indita Pillakul Yenave Magvanung

Vikak Yedung Ovval Takatote Anang
Masal Kurtin Tertan Mangeng
Magvan Kurten Sivval Koreng
Indita Pillakul Yenave Magvanung

Sadi, Zampor, Biryal, Kotva Anung
Masal Maregtin yellat Aneng
Magvan Kurten Kolamanet haus Purepeng
Masal Kuritin Karbharal
Magvan Adnet Bhadeta Hellang

Inangi Masasil Ijjav Magvanung
Sukhamungsathi Dhotarnilepav Magvanung

The married girls of today ask their husbands to bring water in big pots. Thus the girls become masters and husbands do work under them. At times the girls ask them to bring fuelwood from the forest, at times they ask them to cook. If the body of girls is aching, they even ask the husband to massage their bodies. They even ask him to purchase saree, blouse and silver finger rings for the legs.

The song depicts how the modern girls behave with their husbands.

A Modern Song : Indicating Social Change

This song is composed by an educated Kolam youth Shriram Zode, Poet, who urges the parents to educate their wards and keep a watch on them.

Shalata Kolava Balakul (Kolam boys go to school)

Kolava Balakul Kandar Shala
Nalummati Aanar Kulti Aala
Ghorippatna Tinar Kakatna Veta
Derrojtad Avaret Iddi Ata

Okko Jir-Shalang Sare Raja
Master Veltolten te Bheltehi Maja
Yenar Yebtarung Master Kankejja
Inang Idakadung wa-toted Lajja

Vinanti Katna Iddatun Ban-Bekung
Inneltanat Shalang Pankur Balakulang

Yejil Dokali Shalang Koseser Aavrung
Sinnamtanli Gottikul Iddur

Duniyan Ola Batteng Iddur
Aai Bai Ne Walung Pankur Shalang
Karpata – Shivaya Sudharildatun Yenanang ?
Bainev Karapatevete Sudharipav Yellang
Iddi Sudharilakad Killi Andad
Shriram Vinanti Ka Andan Yena
Iddi Patanet Sar Anda Yena
Karpatna Ir Sudharilur Yena

Boys from Kolam community go to the school. While going, they play games and also do hunting and killed animals. If the teacher asks, they are in a fix. Then they say that the teacher abuses their parents.

Hence I request the parents to keep a watch. And see whether they go to the school or not, also whether they study are not. Unless the boys are educated, poverty cannot go.

Teach good things to your children and ask them to see how the world is changing.

I also humbly request my mothers and ladies that there is scope for progress. But we must send our daughters to school without which they cannot progress. If the girls are progressive the whole household can be progressive.

Hence I earnestly request you all to send your sons and daughters to school.

Other Songs

These songs are sung while cutting grass and taking out the bark of trees.

They go to the forest dancing and while the men remove the bark of trees, the women bundle the grass and bark. The following songs are sung during these operations.

Song sung while cutting grass

This song is sung while cutting grass–

Man : Ghaddi Arkeng Baikul Wattir ?
Women : Tane Raj Siyativ Dada ?

M.	Aatana Roj Siyatun, Baikul
W.	Rojal Wattume, Dada
M.	Ghaddi Arkeng Chandur, Baikul
W.	Ed Pav Sennare Dada
M.	Ine Mena Cham, Baikul
W.	Bonda Pav Senar, Dada
M.	Ine Mena Cham, Baikul
W.	Bejja Gettal Biyav, Dada
M.	Ine Mena Cham Baikul
W.	Male Pav Senar, Dada
M.	Ine Mena Cham Baikul
W.	Bejja Khedel Mungav, Dada
M.	Ine Mena Cham Baikul

This is a conversation between a man and women.

M.	O Women, come for cutting grass ?
W.	Dada, How much money will you give us ?
M.	O Women, I will pay eight Annas (fifty paise) per day
W.	Dada, we will come for wages
M.	O Women, Let's go for cutting grass
W.	Dada which way shall we go
M.	O Women, go by any way you wish
W.	Shall we go by the road on the lower side ?
M.	O Women go by the road you wish

This song is sung while they go to bazaar by dancing.

Man :	Angadi Kakur Baikl, Angadi
Women :	Angadi Katume Dada, Angadi
M.	Wadi Wadi Kakure Baikul
W.	Wadi Wadi Kakatame Dada
M.	Urung Chandu re Baikul
W.	Urung Wattung Dada
M.	Wadi Wadi Chandure Baikul
W.	Ine Venkat Watte Dada
M.	Urung Wattame baikul

Meaning

M.	O Women, lets go for bazaar.
W.	O Dada, we go for the bazaar.
M.	O Women hurry up.
W.	O Dada, we are hurrying up.
M.	O Women, Let's return to our village.
W.	O Dada, we come to our village.
M.	O Women, hurry up for going to the village.
W.	O Dada, we are following you.
M.	O Women, we have returned to our village.

This song is sung while bundling the grass after grass-cutting is over–

Women.	Thada Nara Bejja Piddur Dada
Men.	Mopul Yena Perpur Eh Baikul
W.	Mopul Perptan Dada
M.	Tiva Tiva Kattur Baikul
W.	Tiva Tiva Kattame Dada
M.	Moplena Kutture Baikul
W.	Moplena Kuttame Dada
M.	Waeiwadi Chandur Baikul
W.	Wani Mak Uttin Dada
M.	Mopul Dipur Baikul
W.	Mopul Diptame Dada
W.	Beja Ir Athatan Dada
M.	Tap Ira Salure Baikul
W.	Tap Ira Saltam Dada
M.	Irena Unur Eh Baikul
W.	Irena Undame Dada
W.	Bejja Salle Takad Dada
M.	Aaid Zokal Ungure Baikul
W.	Zararara Zoka Eh Dada
M.	Urung Chandure Baikul
W.	Urungena Wattane Dada
M.	Savadi Muttad Pav Chandure Baikul
W.	Wani Lajja Wahad Dada
M.	Addam Kong Kakkev Baikul
W.	Addam Kong Kaktane Dada

M.	Mopul Rusyur Baikul
W.	Mopul Rusitam Eh Dada

After cutting grass they come to the village and then try to take out the bark of different trees. The following discussion takes placed between the men and women.

Women :	Dada this bark is very sticky.
Man :	O Women try to bundle the bark properly.
W.	O Dada we have made the bundles of the bark.
M.	O Women tie them firmly.
W.	O Dada we have tied the bundle firmly.
M.	O Women take the bundle on your heads.
W.	O Dada we have taken the bundles on our head.
M.	O Women start quickly.
W.	O Dada our necks have become heavy due to burden.
M.	O Women keep the bundles down.
W.	O Dada we have kept the bundles down.
W.	O Dada we are thirsty.
M.	O Women dig 'wells', in the sand on the river bank.
W.	O Dada we have prepared 'wells'.
M.	O Women drink water.
W	O Dada we are drinking water.
W.	O Dada the water is very cold.
M.	O Women Let's take five strokes on the proper roots.
W.	O Dada we are taking strokes.
M.	O Women Let's go to the town.
W.	O Dada we have come to the town.
M.	O Women Let's go by the way near *Chavdi.*
W.	O Dada we feel shy.
M.	Then take the end of your saree on your face.
W.	O Dada we have taken the end of saree on face.
M.	O Women keep the bundles down.
W.	O Dada we have kept the bundles down.

Children Songs

While playing, the children sing this song

Aammaya Aamban, Aangadi Sedden
Aame Ellata, Sinkudi Puyatin
Aatane – Futane, Tumaki – Khutane
Sitta Tatun, Ghurral Battev
Tule Tule Papi
Pesar Paap Pong Tula,
Tule Tule Papi

Our parents (mother and father) have gone to bazaar.

On the top of our house flowers have come on the creeper *Val. Phutane bitane* and the pole of tembhurni tree.

Horses have come below the tamarind tree.

Boiling pulse is spilling out the pulse of *Mung* is spilling out, the pulse is spilling out.

The above song is sung by children while playing.

Hunting Songs

The Peacock Song (Goodinine Lovang)

This song is sung at the time of hunting and is a chorus song –

Guddine Lovag Lamani Seddine
Eh Deva Lala !
Guddine Lovag Lamani Seddine
Dhobaketa Lamani Venkaye
Eh Deva Lala !
Dhobakeka Lamani Venkaye
Dhobakune Guddi Tinade
Eh Deva Lala !
Dhobakune Guddi Tinade
Dhoggi Dhoggi Lamani Tulade
Eh Deva Lala !
Dhoggi Dhoggi Lamani Tulade
Dhobakeka Lamani Venkaye
Eh Deva Lala !
Dhobakeka Lamani Venkaye

Sumeng Sedden Te Toka Puttin
Goleg Yena Sedden Te
Moda Kinitin !
Eh Deva Lala !
Goleg Yena Sedden Te
Moda Kinitin

The peacock has entered the valley of bears, O my God !

The peacock has entered the valley of bears following the grandfather, O my God !

The peacock has followed the grandfather, the bear will now eat the grandfather, O my God !

The bear will now eat the grandfather, the peacock ran with long jumps, O my God !

The peacock ran with long jumps, and came following the grandfather, O my God !

The peacock came following the grandfather, when he tried to catch the tail, the tail broke away. When he tried to beat with a stick, the stick broke away, O my God ! the stick broke away.

Literary Criticism

A reading of the folk-songs of the Kolam tribals indicates that they are on the style of Gondi songs and also contain many Gondi words. Due to their proximity with the Pardhan tribals, influence of the Pardhan culture is also obvious.

A rough classification of the songs collected shows that they can be classified into songs with traditional themes and modern themes. The traditional themes include the ritual songs or the *Pooja* songs which are in praise of their traditional Gods and Goddesses. These deities often simulate those of the Gonds and Pardhans. The *Pooja* items or material mentioned in the songs are also common with other tribals or even non- tribals, for example *coconut (Narial), Sindur (Shendur), Bukka, Ral, Camphor etc.*

The other traditional songs pertain to marriage and relationship between husband and wife. The teasing between the bride's party and the groom's party is very common. Similarly, the husband trying to persuade or please the wife by offering to purchase things for her, are also common. The marriage ceremony itself is an occasion on which small sonnets are often composed.

The other class of traditional songs is related to the occupation of farming, grass-cutting, fuel-wood collection etc. The women working as labourers and the men who guide their work – exchange funny words and carry on conversation so as to ease the tension of work. In these songs we find references to trees, animals and many other things from Nature.

There are some songs, primarily made for the children who help in farming operations. These have little meaning and are just for children's fun.

A few hunting songs are given. These include references to animals and birds and are chorus songs. They are meant to keep up the morale of the hunting group and to create noise in the forest.

There are a few songs with spiritual orientation. These songs indicate the perishable nature of the human being and of the earthly pleasures and teach that people should follow the teachings of the saints in their lives.

Another class of songs is of the modern songs based on modern themes. Some of these are composed by educated Kolams. These songs describe the importance of education and urge the parents to send their children to school. Similarly, in one song a modern educated girl is compared to a traditional girl showing that the modern girls become the masters and their husbands have to work in the house under them.

On the whole the Kolam folk-literature includes traditional folk songs in it, contrary to the opinion expressed by some earlier scholars that their dialect is not rich in folk literature. The themes in their songs are also varied. However, as compared to the Gonds and Pardhans the themes and subject matter do not contain the variety of themes which is found in the folk literature of these other tribes. Similarly, the literary content and figures of speech or the ornamentation of the language is not found in their songs. It is pure and simple with a down-to-earth approach. Similarly, in many other tribes like the Gonds and Pardhans or the Korku there are songs containing references to the origin of their tribe, social organisation and ordering of the society etc. Such songs are not available in those collected by different scholars. It is very likely that the researchers so far, could not collect such songs, or that the Kolams do not have such songs. One of the reasons may be that the Kolam tribe being ethnically akin to the Gonds (particularly the Naik-Gonds), did not have separate tales or mythology on which such songs could be composed. Briefly, though the Kolam's dialect does contain folk-literature, the present stage of collection indicates that it is not as extensive and rich as that of the Gonds, Pardhans or other tribes in the vicinity.

Dances

Dandar dances are most popular among the Kolams of the Yavatmal and Nanded districts. At the time of the *Gaon-Bandhani* ritual a typical type of Dandar is performed in which *Ghusadi* or *Gosai*, who are the spiritual leaders of the community/*Pujari* take the lead. The local Patel or Naik inaugurates this dance and some rituals follow. A teen-age boy plays the role of "Kodyal" and is not allowed to return home till the whole Dandar season is over. During the dance the Ghusadis put on an attractive make-up and walk with a *Danda* (Rod) or some weapon like a sword in hand and dance outside the circle of the Dandar dancers and when the Dandar moves from village to village, the Ghusadi is the 'vanguard' for the procession and provides protection. After the Dandar is over, only the Ghusadis dance when they are possessed with the spirits.

Another dance which is performed as an interlude between the Dandar dances is called *Ghorpadi* dance (Ghorpad means *iguana*). This represents the age-old tribal nature of imitating the Nature. The dancers who are always in pairs imitate *Ghorpad* and dance lying prostrate on ground, on palms and foot-fingers, and moving in the posture of peacock (Magurusan) on the tunes of music. This looks as a terrible difficult dance and is performed by a few persons only.

The various things used during the dances as costume include the bark of trees, feathers of peacock, animal skins and, of late, towels or handkerchiefs are used in lieu of the above articles. Occasionally, a torch is also held in one hand and a stick or a danda in the other hand.

The instruments used for music include flute made from bamboo (*Bansuri* or *Vansh*), *Turbudi* and Drums. *Turbudi* is prepared from the skin of a goat and is used like a *Daf*. Many other instruments are being adopted from other tribes or from the modern world depending upon their association with the outside world.

Liquor, particularly the *Mahua* liquor is consumed during all dances and rituals.

Musical Instruments

As dancing and singing are very common, various musical instruments are also used. These include *Daf, Paul, Dholak, Chonak*, etc.

Daf is prepared locally by Kolam. Its body is prepared from the trunk of a tree (Tamarind tree) which is as big in circumference as that of a wheel of a cycle while leather of the goat is fitted on the body.

Paul is prepared from bamboo and is a flute type instrument.

The *Dholak* and *Chonak* are prepared by the usual method from the non-tribal world or may be purchased.

Dances are performed at the time of *Gaon-Bandhani, Bhivsan-Aanghol, Holi, Dushera, Diwali* and also on marriage occasions. The songs are composed by the people themselves and are either about the Gods or the ritual/the festivals or containing humour teasing etc. The whole community participates in dancing and singing. The dancing styles are mostly based on rhythm and hence vary according to the instruments used. Consumption of liquor is an essential aspect of all these dances.

Kolami Words
Words Showing Numerals

English	*Kolami*
One	Okkon, Okkod
Two	Indig
Three	Muyyal
Four	Naling
Five	Pach, Ayda
Six	Saha
Seven	Sat
Eight	Aatha
Nine	Nav
Ten	Daha
Eleven	Akra
Fifteen	Pendara
Nineteen	Eakunis
Twentyone	Eakvis
Eighty	Ansi

Words Showing Animals

English	*Kolami*
Rat	Elka
Camel	Lotti
Dog	Aate
Jackal	Kolyak
A Crab	Ende

English	*Kolami*
Deer	Gorya/Pot gorya
An ass	Gaddi
Monkey	Mutha
Cow	Kute
Crocodile	Mosali
Bandicot rat	Ghushi
Horse	Gurram
Musk-rat	Shisudrak
Pig	Turre
He-goat	Bokodyak
She-goat	Meke
Heron	Beglyak
Panther	Bibtyak
He-cat	Potpilli

Words Showing Trees

English	*Kolami*
Cotton	Karve
Chironjee	Shire mak
Tamarind	Sitta
Jamun	Jamre
Toddy Palm	Shindibonda, Tadamak
Papaiya	Popoyi
Palas	Modgumak
Pipple	Ravi
Mahua	Hirip
Lemon	Nimbu

Words Showing Colour

English	*Kolami*
Black	Dondak
Red	Lal
White	Telmi/Yerodi
Yellow	Pisudi

English	Kolami
Blue	Tevvak
Pale Green	Hirvat

Words Showing Parts of the Body

English	Kolami
Head	Tal
Eye	Kan
Nose	Mungad/Sudi Bogga
Ear	Kev
Lip	Pedawe
Cheeks	Pukli
Throat	Dodor
Hand	Kiya
Leg	Getta/Kal
Finger	Vende
Stomach	Potta
Thumb	Angtha
Small finger	Sir-Vende
Forehead	Kapar
Waist	Tikane
Hair	Tir
Mouth	Moti
Palm	Tara
Shoulder	Bujam/Satta
Knee	Tonge
Tongue	Nalka

Words Showing Relationship

English	Kolami
Mother	Amma/Takama
Step Mother	Napa Amma
Father	Tak/Ban
Brother	
Sister	Tondarl
Father's elder brother	Don Ban

English	*Kolami*
Mother's elder sister	Dobek
Grand-father	Donban/Dhoba
Grand-mother	Budyaban
	Murtalbek
Grand-Son/Daughter	Marage/Marge
Father's Sister	Appa
Daughter-in-Law	Koral
Mother's Brother	Mamak
Mother's younger sister	Sanma
Mother's sister's husband	Kakok
Father's Brother	Kakok
Boy	Kike
Daughter's husband	Eltam-Sangin

Words Showing Birds

English	*Kolami*
Bird	Zaware
Crow	Kaka
Pigeon	Bori/Kebutar
Tortoise	Kanwwe
Indian cuckoo	Kokilak
Cock	Pot
Eagle	Gadda/Morghar
Lapwing	Tewwak
	Parvyak
Parrot	Mituk
Butterfly	Guge
Jungle cock	Aadavipot

REFERENCES

1. Karve, Irawati, *Marathi Lokanchi Sanskriti*, R.J. Deshmukh & Co., 1962 (2nd Ed.), Pune, p. 105.
2. Grierson, G.A., *Linguistic Survey of India, Munda and Dravidian Lanugaes*, Vol. IV, p. 561.
3. Russel and Hiralal, *Tribes and Castes of Central Provinces of India*, Cosmo

Publications, Delhi 1961 (Reprint) 1975, p. 522.

4. Mandaokar, Bhau, *Kolam*, Seva Prakashan, Amravati, 1966 pp. 308-9.
5. *Ibid*; pp. 309-10.
6. *Ibid*; pp. 311-12.
7. *Ibid*; p. 313.

9. Kolam Tribals near Maroti Mandir — Lambori (Korapna)

10. Godess Marai, Palan

11. Vishnu Mandir, in the Vallies of Manikgarh

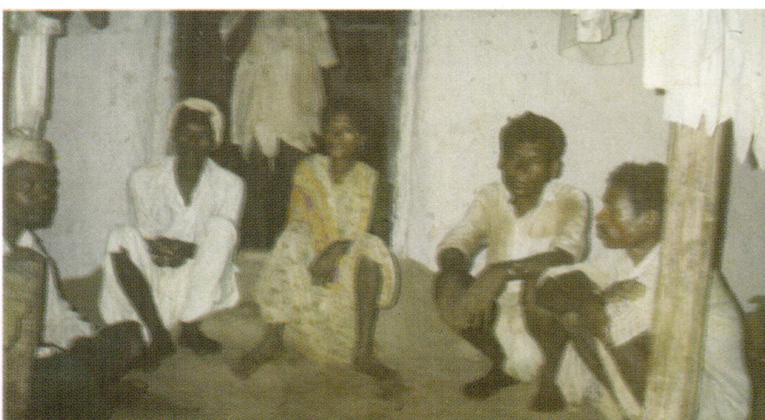

12. A Kolam Group: Ambezari

13. Chikhliguda: A Typical Kolam Village

14. Kolam Women with their Childern — Chikhliguda

15. A Marriage 'Mund' Ambezari

16. A Typical Kolam Woman. Lambori

17. Kolams in '*Ghusadi Dance*' at Nokewada (Tah. Korapna)

18. Ghusadi and Kolam Women Dance at Nokewada (Tah. Korapna)

19. Ghusadis and Kolam Women in a dance

20. Gusadis dancing

21. A Kolam dancing in costume to the tune of *Duf* and Flute at Mokadumguda (Tah. Korapna)

5

POLITICAL ORGANISATION AND ADMINISTRATION OF JUSTICE*

Village Organisation

In a Kolam *Pod* there is a Panchayat (Council of Five, though there are only four office-bearers) which looks after the organisational function as well as judicial functions. The Kolams submit to its jurisdiction rather than approaching to the state police and judiciary. Office-bearers of the Council are Naik, Mahajan, Karbhari, Ghatya.

Naik

It is the most powerful office. He is respected by all. He is chief of the *Pod*. He plays a key role in meetings, community functions, festivals and gets precedence on such occasions. His decision is respected and order obeyed. Usually he himself does not decide cases without consultation with other office-bearers and the community members. He cannot act contrary to common good and the Pod as a whole keeps watch over him.

Mahajan

He is next to Naik. Mahajan presides over meeting if Naik is absent. At times, in some villages both the posts are held by the same person. He performs same functions as that of Naik's and is respected by all.

---

* This chapter has been contributed by Advocate Leena Deogaonkar and is based on her dissertation.

Karbhari

He is like Secretary of Panchayat. He manages financial as well as other administrative functions. He collects contributions, keeps accounts and makes suggestions to the Panchayat.

Ghatya

He is like a *chaparshi (peon)*. He functions like a messenger. He makes announcements, serves invitations, collects fines etc. He informs the whereabouts of absent persons to the Panchayat.

The term *ghatya* originates from *Ghat*. In marriage ceremony he looks after the "Ghat" (the pious earthen pots full of water) and is highly respected during marriage ceremony.

Tarma

Tarma works as a cook in any public programme organised by the village Panchayat. He also makes announcements regarding public meetings and extends invitation to the villagers.

Traditional Panchayat and its Office-Bearers

In all Kolam *Pods*, there exists the traditional tribal *Panchayat*. It is termed as Panchayat or at times *Nyaya Panchayat*. The meetings of the Panchayat are held in the *Chavdi*. It is a meeting place for all community functions. Naik, Mahajan, Karbhari and Ghatya are the four office-bearers of the Panchayat. They are elected by the people.

The *Chavdi* has an open place where the meetings are held. All people, usually, sit in semicircle. Everyone has right to speak and is provided with an opportunity to express one's views freely. Once decision is arrived at, all are duty bound to obey it. Fines are the most common punishment that is inflicted on wrong doers. Those who do not obey Panchayat decisions are outcasted. Panchayat decides dates for community functions and festivals.

Tarma, Diyakun (*Pujari*), Palchil Neykun (*Chief-Naik*) are some of the posts which may exist. But these are not necessarily filled in all *Pods*. None of the above posts (including that of Panchas) are occupied by ladies. Traditionally, they are not allowed to hold these posts.

Process of Election

On the day of *Gudi Padwa* (or a day earlier or later) all men-folk of the *Pod* assemble at *Chavdi*. If people are satisfied with existing office-bearers and their functioning then the confidence is reposed in them unequivocally. But if their functioning is not thought to be satisfactory or due to any other reason the old Panchas are to be removed, then elections are held. Usually, Panchas are elected by consensus. A betel leaf and nut are placed at the centre and persons are encouraged or discouraged by people to pick it up. This shows backing or opposition to the person.

If the person occupying the post of Naik dies before completing the post tenure, then the post remains in his house and his widow enjoys the respect of *Naikin* (wife of the deceased Naik) till the end of the term, though she cannot act as Naik. Then fresh body is elected. The election is taken by voice-vote *i.e.* a name is proposed for the post, if he is acceptable to all then he is deemed to be elected. All persons can have a say, and it carries equal weightage. If there arises any difference of opinion, elderly people are consulted and their suggestions are taken into account. Then such elected persons are presented with betel leaf (*Wida*) and coconut and a rupee or two as a mark of respect (*Dakshina*).

Functions of the Panchas

Naik is the head of the Panchayat. Naik decides how to proceed with work. Left to himself Naik alone does not perform any function. He, along with three other office-bearers performs the duties and functions.

Though disputes are resolved by all the men of the *Pod*, these Panchas (particularly Naik and Mahajan), take initiative in the process.

They assemble and fix the dates of cultural functions like *Gaon-Bandhani* (Religious Fortification of the *Pod*). They also collect the contributions for that purpose. Karbhari acts as a Secretary. He keeps the accounts, spends money accordingly. Ghatya does all manual work. He calls the people for meetings, makes public announcements, carries messages etc.

Panchayat also settles marriages. Worshipping God, preserving the culture and tradition of the village are some of the functions of the Panchas in addition to the above.

Functioning of the Traditional Panchayat

The Panchas do the work of dispensing justice. But decision is arrived at by the method of consensus. Elderly persons discuss the matter. Both the parties are allowed to plead their sides. If there is any contradiction in narration of the party, the fault is detected.

Usually, the basis of delivering judgements is found in the traditional norms and customs handed down from generation to generation. What traditions are binding is decided by Panchas and other elder members of the community.

The Panchas and other elderly persons assemble at *Chavdi*. Both the parties are allowed to plead their sides.

After both sides are heard, the Panchas arrive at a decision. The decision is made by consensus. The Panchas consult the elderly and wise people present at *Chavdi*.

While narrating the incident, if the persons baffle, the fault may be detected; and the decision is arrived at by the consensus method.

If there arises any difference of opinion among the Panchas, the *Aam-sabha* of the whole *Pod* is called. All elderly persons and the folk deliberate and strike a solution to the problem.

For small, petty offences the offender is merely warned and asked to behave properly. Fines depending upon the offences, are inflicted. Fines are the most common way of punishing an offender. The money so collected by way of fines is used for common good.

If the decision is not obeyed by the parties they are beaten by the Panchas and others. Social boycott is also a common method observed. But if the majority of the people are not ready to comply with the Panchas' orders, the splinter group forms other *Pod.*

An appeal is heard by the *Aamsabha* of the whole village. Traditionally, ladies are not allowed to participate in the Panchayat proceedings except where she has to depose before the Panchayat.

Naik keeps the supervision, vigilance over the functioning of the Panchayat. And the community as a whole keeps watch over the Panchas. If their functioning is not thought satisfactory, they are not re-elected.

Naik is the most respected person. Mahajan is next to Naik and performs his duties and functions in the absence of Naik. Karbhari is the Secretary-cum-treasurer and looks after the financial matters. Ghatya does all manual work and at the time of marriage; looks after *Ghat* (a sacred pot containing water) which explains the genesis of his post's name.

Bhagat and *Pujari* are consulted in the matters of calamities which are supposed to be due to displeasure of the Goddess and in health matters. The Sarpanch of Gram Panchayat is also respected in his own sphere and consulted for certificates and other developmental activities.

The traditional Panchayat has jurisdiction over all matters, disputes etc. arising in the *Pod* except where one of the parties is an outsider or stranger (*i.e.* a non-Kolam).

The common meeting of all Panchayats of neighbouring Kolam (villages) *Pods* may also be held which decides the policy matters regarding topics of community interest.

Approaching the traditional Panchayat is a rule and deviating from it and taking recourse to modern police and courts is an exception. But due to spread of education younger generation is approaching the Courts and the tradition abiding tendency is fading.

Ladies do not participate in the proceedings of the Panchayat. If some people do not obey orders of the Panchas then they are outcasted. It was so reported by the people, that at times if the splinter group is big then they even form separate *Pod*. That is the reason why sometimes we find 2-3 *Pods* attached to the single village.

Kinds of Punishment

For different offences punishments are different. But, fines are the most common form of punishment inflicted. For small petty offences offender is merely warned to behave properly. The amount of fines differs from offence to offence. The punishment is implemented by the Panchas.

The fine is collected by the Panchayat, particularly Karbhari keeps the account. The amount varies from Rs. 5 to Rs. 100. In cases of severe offences like rape etc., occasionally, the fine of Rs. 500 or above may be imposed. The Kolams believe that it has deterrent effect on the people. The money so collected is used for common good like tea, party and refreshment *e.g.* jaggery and puffed rice (*Murmure*) etc. are distributed to all the people or amount is used for religious functions etc.

If any of the parties does not comply with the Panchayat decision he is beaten by all or else boycotted. Once the fines are paid, the person is exonerated. In the *Pod*, there is no authority above the Panchayat.

False complaints are normally not lodged. But if lodged, such a complainant is warned not to behave in the manner dangerous to the community.

Supervision on the Functions of the Panchas

The Panchas are respected by the community. But they do not get any remuneration either in cash or in kind for the services rendered. At times, Naik himself has to entertain guests and spend accordingly. The community as a whole keeps watch over the functioning of the Panchayat. If they are not found working properly, they are not re-elected.

Arbitration

As it is not prestigious to take recourse even to the traditional Panchayat, the compromise between the parties is tried before approaching to the Panchayat. Elderly persons act as arbitrators and try to bring parties together. In this process, if settlement is arrived at, then the punishments are not inflicted.

Religious Impact

Religious leaders like *Supadi*, *Ghusadi*, *Bhagat*, *Pujari* usually do not participate in delivering judgements. They are only consulted like other people. Their opinion is not very relevant so far as dispensation of justice is concerned. The Panchas have higher position in the traditional judicial set-up. Religious leaders are consulted only in matters of health and other private matters.

All men and women do not assemble at *Chavdi*. Ladies are not allowed to participate in the meetings. But, on very rare occasions, such as religious functions, ladies are present. If a woman is a party to the dispute she has to be present there.

Appeals

If a complainant or any party is not satisfied with the decision of the Panchas (office-bearers) he may approach the whole village community and place his appeal before them.

For settling issues involving policy matters a common meeting of Panchayats of two or more *Pods* may also be convened.

If there arises a dispute between persons from two different *Pods*, the meeting is held in a place which belongs to neither of the *Pod*. Naiks from both the *Pod* preside over the meeting.

There is an instance of one such meeting which was held to decide the legality of marriage between man and woman of different *Pods*.

The meeting of twelve *Pods* was also held where the subjects of common interest were discussed like the inclination towards dowry and continuation of bride-price, its relevance and necessity was itself questioned. Such bodies do have appellate authority; they are so recognised by the people but reportedly people do not approach to it normally.

Usually, if there is any difference of opinion among the Panchayat members that point is ultimately and finally settled by the whole community.

Utilization of Modern Judiciary

Traditional system is utilized and they do not go to modern courts because the traditional system is less expensive, ensures speedy trial and is also favourable to emotional and cultural set-up of tribals. Occasionally, they come into contact with police and courts. For obvious reasons, the experience which they have is not favourable. It is a general belief in Kolami village that a wise and sane person does not approach the police and courts. Only in cases where the other party is a non-Kolam, the case may go to the modern courts when the Kolam may have no option.

Typical Cases

One Jayawant Masram of Kolam *Pod* at Mangli who has passed S.S.C. Examination and was a member of the Statutory Gram Panchayat narrated a typical case from his family. Out of his two daughters, the younger one whose age (at that time) was below 16 years developed a love affair with a Kolam boy from the same village and went to live with him. As per tradition the marriage had to be settled before Panchayat. During the deliberations though all of them okayed the marriage, a difference of opinion developed regarding the actual performance of the marriage ceremony. The girl's father insisted upon performing the ceremony on a grand scale like that in the modern society. While the Panchayat and the boy's party insisted upon the traditional and simple performance. The girl's father resisted, as a result of which the negotiations could not be settled. Rather than following the decision of the Panchayat the girl's father lodged a complaint at the Warora Police Station complaining against the boy and an offence was registered against the boy as the girl living with him was under 16 years of age. The boy was arrested creating a commotion in the Kolam community. The Panchayat met again and boycotted the family of the girl's father for disobeying the decision of the Panchayat and carrying the matters to the court.

In yet another case reported from Pijdura, a boy who is the only double graduate (B.A., B.Ed.) from all the three establishments of the Kolam in Warora Tehsil of Chandrapur district, married a Kolam girl. The marriage was okayed by all but the dispute developed over the style and performance of the marriage. While this boy wanted to combine the good aspects from the traditional style with those of the modern style the Panchayat members insisted upon strictly following the traditional style which emphasises dancing, singing, feast and liquor etc. The boy did not concede, and married according to his wishes, inviting the wrath of the Panchayat. As a result, he and his family were boycotted by the Panchayat. In this case the matter was not (and naturally could not) be carried to the police or the courts but tensions developed in the community.

The third case reported from Mangli is about a widow who lodged a complaint with the police station as someone encroached upon the farm of her dead husband and the matter could not be amicably settled.

In a recent development, some persons from the Paradhi community (a Nomadic tribe who had come to stay on the outskirts of the Mangli village), started tilling the land which was reportedly given to them by the Sarpanch of Mangli (who is a non-Kolam). As a result, the Kolams who were uptill now tilling it, clashed with the Pardhis. The Pardhis lodged a complaint with the Warora Police Station and about 21-25 Kolams were arrested and later released on bail.

By way of conclusion it can be said that the cases from Kolam *Pod* are carried to Police and Court under the following two situations:

1. When the person is educated and is reluctant to follow the outdated traditions and wants to effect a cultural change due to the impact of modern civilization he falls out of the community traditions and if the break-away point also touches statutes or laws he may carry it to the courts or else bravely face the boycott of the panchayat still championing the cause of modernity. The first two cases are a testimony to this fact.
2. In some cases the matter in dispute is concerned with land rights, revenue matters etc., which fall outside the purview/ jurisdiction of the traditional Panchayat or the other parties to the dispute or conflict are not from the Kolam community. In such cases, the other party may proceed to the police and courts leaving no option for the Kolam but to face it.

Kind of Offences Tried by the Traditional Panchayat

All offences where the persons from the Kolams themselves are involved and tried by the traditional Panchayat. These include the following:

1. *Matrimonial Matters*
   Torture to women; rape etc.
   Divorce matters only if carried by the parties to the Panchayat. (Panchayat; of its own does not take cognizance of the divorce matters).
2. Causing nuisance; hurt; grievous hurt.
3. *Murder*— They do not disclose the cause of death, and try to avoid the case. But later the murderer is tried in traditional Panchayat and punished.
4. *If the person disobeys the traditions* at the time of *Gaon-Bandhani*, he is also tried by the Panchayat.
5. A person is not permitted to sale/purchase the house and campus adjoining it to a person other than a Kolam with a view to maintain the integrity of the *Pod.* Thus they are reluctant to allow persons from other community to enter and reside within the habitat of their community.

Where an outsider is involved in a dispute the matter would go to courts *e.g.* accident etc.

People are of the opinion that developmental work must be given to the traditional Panchayat as these are non-corrupt bodies. One ex-Naik was progressive enough to suggest that the bride-price must be abolished and a woman should get equal right of inheritance in the estate of the father.

Traditional Panchayat and the People's Interaction with it

Every-one replied in affirmative, when asked whether there exists traditional Panchayat in the Kolam *Pod.* This shows awareness of all about its existence.

About the functions of the Panchayat, various functions were enumerated by the respondents. These are as under:–

a) Social, economic and religious problems;
b) Dispensation of Justice;

c) Maintenance of peace and order;
d) Functions pertaining to marriage, settlement of marriage and the terms thereof;
e) Financial help to the needy.
f) Religious affairs: So far as the religious functions are concerned the role of Panchayat is to take decisions regarding celebrations, the actual performance at the community level and such other policy matters.
g) The Office-bearers take initiative at such functions, *e.g.*—The *Gaon-Bandhani* etc.

All Kolams were found to be aware of the office-bearers of the traditional Panchayat and the names of the present incumbent of the posts.

Kolam men answered in affirmative, when asked whether they come into contact with the traditional Panchayat. Those who answered negatively were also ready to accept the jurisdiction of the Panchayat. As some people were boycotted by the Panchayat, they were not allowed to attend it. But Kolam women reportedly do not come into contact with the Panchayat for various reasons. These are as follows:

a) Traditionally they are not allowed to participate in the proceedings;
b) As all men-folk sit there, the women avoid going to the Panchayat, unless extremely essential, *i.e.* in connection with a dispute.

It was reported by all that the whole community comes in contact with the Panchayat on occasions which are celebrated on community level *e.g.*—worshipping the Deities, marriage ceremonies, settling marriages, dances and feasts incidental to marriage. All the male members along with the Panchayat members assemble and come in contact with each other at the time of *Aam-sabha* (*i.e.* meeting of the whole community), Panchayat meeting, *Nyaya Panchayat*, *i.e.* when the Panchayat sits for settling disputes.

Settlement of Disputes

It was stated that the disputes are settled amicably between the parties by personal negotiations when they are petty disputes, but they may use the good offices of some elderly person *i.e.* through arbitration.

In case this does not help, the dispute is taken to the Panchayat which deliberate and gives decision by consensus which is normally accepted by the parties concerned.

Those disputes which are neither domestic nor petty are carried before the Panchayat. These include—

i) Disputes regarding cruelty and injustice;
ii) Fights between persons, beating and thrashing each other;
iii) Cruel and in-human treatment to women, molestation, rape, etc. and the problems regarding improvident pregnancy of unmarried girls;
iv) Severe quarrels between spouses;
v) About divorce matters;
vi) About bride-price and dowry; and
vii) To check and punish socially harmful behaviour of persons.

Some Kolams from the younger generation stated that due to decline in blind-faith and also in the traditions and customs the youths are not eager to take their disputes to the Panchayat. A discordant note was also perceptible between the elderly office-bearers and the youths in these villages on such issues.

Administration of Justice in the Kolam

The concept of law prevailing in different tribes in the customary and traditional code of conduct is handed down from generation to generation. It is a part of their socio-cultural heritage. In some of the tribes, the Tribal Councils are adequate and efficient to give everyone his due. It commands tribal allegiance. It has done commendable work in maintaining peace and for keeping the tribe united.

It was thus found that the Kolams have their own separate traditional system of administration of justice.

Characteristics of the Traditional Panchayat of Kolams

Though it is called as Panchayat which literally means 'a council of five', there are only four office-bearers *viz.* Naik, Mahajan, Karbhari, Ghatya.

Chavdi is a place where all community functions including the meeting of the Panchayat are held.

Democratic functioning of the Panchayat is the main and dominant characteristic. 'Consensus method' of arriving at any decision is a striking feature. It shows how democratic ideas are deep-rooted in the tribal population. It is in a real sensė; 'the Panchayat by the people, for the people and of the people'.

Elections are held every year. There are no hereditary posts. The office-bearers do not get any remuneration. On the contrary, the Naik himself has to spend for the guests of the *Pod* from his own pocket. This shows how community spirit is present amongst the people.

The office-bearers cannot and do not hold the posts against the wishes of the people neither can they reject to hold it if the community persuades them to do so.

Without written codes, without any formal system, the Panchayat decision is accepted, obeyed and the compliance therewith is made.

For non-compliance, a system of punishment exists. The fine collected by way of punishment is utilised for common good. If the decision is not accepted by majority, then they split and form another *Pod.*

Thus on the whole, the prominent thing which can be observed is that public benefit is of supreme importance. Common good of the community prevails over individual good. The 'real will' always takes precedence over the 'actual will'.

Naturally to preserve these valuable traditions even a slight deviation from traditional to modern behaviour is criticised and taken note of.

After studying the administration of Justice in tribal communities, of the Chandrapur district and after analysing the data collected the following conclusions are drawn—

1. There do exist systems for administration of justice in the tribal communities.
2. There is an elaborate set-up for the administration of justice in the primitive tribe Kolam which is still in active operation in spite of the fact that these Kolam *Pods* are surrounded by non-tribal modern communities who have a developed modern system of law and courts.
3. Their system has got an independent Panchayat which is a structure elected by the people and an organisation which is linked with the community in the *Pod* in an organic form.
4. Traditionally, for Kolams these structures are formal, because there is a formal election to the post of the

Panchayat, a formal tenure and fixed functions. Though all these things depend upon the unwritten traditions and conventions, however, the procedures followed for the functioning of the Panchayat are non-formal and flexible in nature.

But, for the modern viewer from the developed communities who have got a statutory system of courts and other bodies for dispersing justice, the Kolams' system may seem to be non-formal in nature.

5. The Panchayat is the institution which consists of the four offices *viz*. Naik, Mahajan, Karbhari and Ghatya. *Aamsabha* is the wider institution which is called by the Panchayat as and when the differences of opinion arise amongst the Panchas as it is the ultimate decision-making body of the *Pod*. Common meetings of Panchayats may also be called in cases of disputes between the residents of different *Pods*.
6. Naik is he head of the *Pod* and decides the procedure of the work; and performs the duties attached to his office. Mahajan acts in his absence. Karbhari is the treasurer and looks after finances. Ghatya carries messages and calls the people for meetings.
7. The authorities are a part and parcel of the community and though sharing life with the community command respect precedence and obedience. Their decisions are obeyed and implemented.
8. Customs and traditions as handed down by generations and crystallised into norms form the basis of delivering judgments. In cases of difference on such points the Panchayat and *Aamsabha* define and decide the principles in particular cases.
9. There is no separate machinery for implementing punishments. The office-bearers of the Panchayat and the people from the community themselves implement the punishments, *e.g.* once the fine is imposed, it is deposited with the Karbhari and if the person concerned does not obey, the elderly people or the community people beat him. In cases of boycott the whole community shuns socials relationship with the offender. Here this is an example where deliberative or legislative functions, judicial functions and the executive functions are together in the same body *i.e.* the

Panchayat and the community as the '*Aamsabha*'. All the roles are played as and when necessary.

10. In this sphere *i.e.* the administration of justice, the sacred authorities have little role to play. They are respected only so far as the rituals are concerned, specially worship of Gods and Goddesses and propitiating evil spirits. Even the decisions regarding the performance of such functions, the dates etc. are decided by the Panchayat. If at all there is any role for these sacred authorities, it is only as individuals in the community.

This tribal community which, of late, has been declared as a primitive tribe by the Government, has still maintained the traditional set-up, institutions and methods for the administration of justice which are still functioning in an effective manner and regulating the socio-cultural life of the community. Due to the eloquent failure of our modern law and order and judicial set-up, the harassments suffered by those who avail of it and the rampant corruption and injustice prevailing in it have discouraged these tribals from giving up their traditional system which is relatively more reliable, non-exploitative and fool-proof in delivering justice.

Political Consciousness

The Kolam participate in elections. In most of the returns it was stated that about 90 to 100 per cent voters turn out for voting. But except for their caste panchayat they rarely contest elections. A few have been elected to the statutory Gram Panchayat and even have become Sarpanch. They do not participate or become members of political parties. Hence, at the district or higher levels they have no Kolam leader who can safe-guard their interests. Women of course are more backward in the political sphere.

They have no voluntary social organisations separate from religious organisations. The social interests are taken care of by the traditional village panchayat. They have no association or co-ordination with the tribal leaders from other tribes in the vicinity like the Pardhans and the Gonds. Hence, for solving their problems they miserably lack any spokesman who can discuss or bargain the problems with the government. This results in keeping them backward.

6

ECONOMY AND DEVELOPMENT

Like all other tribals they were hunters and killing wild-pigs was a favourite pass-time. Now this has almost stopped. Originally, the Kolams were living on the mountain slopes. They knew farming but were shifting cultivators and did not plough the land but adopted the broadcast method for sowing seeds like the Gonds. This was called *Podu* which means shifting cultivation.* Later, they adopted traditional method of cultivation with ploughs, axes and crow-bars etc. In many of the villages they are cultivators but their lands are infertile and hence not sufficient for livelihood of their families. Hence many of them started working as labourers on the farms of landlords, while others migrated in search of labour-work. Some of them got wages as forest labourers while others worked hard on stone-cutting by hands. The State Government gave them lands in some areas which was not cultivable. Stone-cutting work was also given to them under the EGS (Employment Guarantee Scheme) of the State Government but due to reported rampant corruption they could not get wages commensurate to their labour. Women also work on farms as labourers along with men.

Some Kolam youths are employed on the farms of landlords with wages in kind (food-grains) and/or in cash which may be a fixed sum.

Making the fallow land cultivable by up-rooting the roots of big trees and shrubs is a difficult job. Many Kolams do this hard labour for earning livelihood.

Bunding of land for irrigation and soil conservation also offers them opportunities for labour work. Digging wells, trenches, etc. is also done by them.

Bamboo work, including making bamboo mats and grain-storage

---

* It is believed by some that the term *Pod* used for Kolam village might be having its origin in *Podu*.

barrels from bamboo is also one of their occupations. Knitting of wooden cots by jute rope strings etc. is done by them.

They also keep herds of goats and cattle for the landlords from the village.

Cutting grass from the forest, collecting fire-wood and selling it is one of the favourite occupations for the Kolams. Some Kolams are working as wood-work artisans.

Very few of them are educated and employed on white-collared jobs but the percentage is negligible.

As we have seen, traditionally, they have been working as labourers and have migrated from place to place for labour work. Of late, their major occupation has been stone-cutting and working as labours on forest-roads or forest. Those Kolams who reside in the forest pick-up minor forest produce like Gum, Honey, Mahua, Flowers, Chironji etc. During the last 50 to 60 years, after they settled down, some of them started keeping cattle and doing some minor daily work.

Some Kolam villages encroached upon forest land and started doing agriculture. These pieces of land vary from 2 to 10 acres depending upon the need and availability. But even today their main source for earning bread has been labour work.

After the commencement of the tribal development schemes some of them obtained goats and she-goats. Hence they started rearing of goats also.

Even after tilling the land for many years they could not get the *pattas* (Title deeds) for the lands, hence in spite of their efforts they are unable to settle down as agriculturist. One of the important reasons is they lack leaders who can effectively present their case to the government or negotiate at the political level. The Project Officers appointed under Integrated Tribal Development Programme are also not taking genuine interest in reaching the benefits of the schemes to these tribals. Except distribution of roofing tiles and electric connection to few houses, other benefits have not been obtained. Even the approach roads to their villages are not negotiable in all seasons. The following complaints and demands were put forth by them during a survey on development.

1. They don't get information about the development schemes in spite of the fact that special officers have been appointed for the purpose.
2. As and when they try to get the benefits under the schemes the official hurdles in the concerned departments obstruct

them from getting the advantages. Due to their ignorance and poverty they are unable to overcome hurdles.

3. They have even reported that some of the officers bargain for getting family planning cases from the tribals as a pre-condition for giving the benefits of the scheme.

They have made the following demands :

1. Better and more lighting for villages and houses in the village.
2. A government fair price shop in the village or in the vicinity which will supply some grocery items in addition to food-grains.
3. Implements, and pair of bullocks with bullock-carts for the farmers.
4. Establishment of a co-operative society for organising the Kolam labour doing stone work.
5. Primary and middle schools within an areas of 10 kms. from the villages with qualified teaching staff.
6. Pure drinking water facilities for each village. The tubewell water is not always potable for health.
7. Appointment of Kolami women/girls as *Anganwadi* workers in the *Anganwadis* in the Kolam villages.
8. Appointment of teachers who know Kolami dialect in the schools around these villages so that in the first two standards the Kolam children can be taught in their mother tongue.
9. As far as possible giving job to at least one person from each Kolam household.
10. Giving more and sufficient loans to the Kolam people who want to start their own business occupation, etc.
11. A few Kolams who are farmers even demanded electric motor pumps for irrigation on their farms.

A typical case may be mentioned here. A Kolam youth who passed B.A. and B.Ed. examinations of the Nagpur University in Second division could not get job. He appeared at interview at Zila Parishad level but was not selected even on the post reserved for scheduled tribes. When he contacted the Collector of the district, the Collector ridiculed him saying that as he was a tribal so he may go on roaming from place to place and should not need a job. When some school gave him a job the concerned education officer raised some technical objection for his appointment as the school was from Gadchiroli district. He was the first and the only double graduate, from the Chandrapur district but was jobless. As a result the other Kolams asked as to why should they send their wards to schools and colleges if this was going to happen. It was only after the present author took up his case with the Secretary, Tribal Development Department at the Secretariat at Bombay, that the things moved and his appointment was okayed.

The facts stated above indicate that much remains to be done for the economic development of this primitive tribe. They have potentials which may be compared well with any other progressive tribal population but as they have no spokesmen for their community they are as yet left just on the banks of the main stream of development and progress.

BIBLIOGRAPHY

Emenue, M.B. 1955, *Kolami – A Dravidian Language*, London

Grierson, G.A. 1906, *Linguistic Survey of India*, Vol. IV (Reprint-1967) Motilal Banarsidas, Calcutta

Karve, Iravati, 1962, *Morathi Lokanchi–Sanskriti*, Deshmukh & Co., Pune

Maharashtra State 1974, *Maharashtra State Gazetteers* – Yavatmal State, Gazetteers Deptt. Bombay.

Mandaokar, Bhau, 1966, *Kolam*, Seva Prakashan, Amravati.

Pagdi Setu – Madhav Rao, 1950, *A Grammar of Kolami Language*, Hyderabad.

Russel, R.V. and Hiralal, 1916, *Tribes and Castes of the Central Provinces of India*, (Reprint-1975) Cosmo Publications, Delhi.

INDEX